SEVEN ESSENTIALS FOR FAMILY-PROFESSIONAL PARTNERSHIPS IN EARLY INTERVENTION

Seven Essentials for Family-Professional Partnerships in Early Intervention

Bonnie Keilty

with contributions by
Hedi Levine and Sagarika Kosaraju

Foreword by Philippa Campbell

Teachers College Press
TEACHERS COLLEGE | COLUMBIA UNIVERSITY
NEW YORK AND LONDON

Published by Teachers College Press, 1234 Amsterdam Avenue, New York, NY 10027

Copyright © 2017 by Teachers College, Columbia University

Cover design by David K. Kessler. Cover photo by USGirl / iStock by Getty Images.

All rights reserved. No part of this publication may be reproduced or transmitted in any form or by any means, electronic or mechanical, including photocopy, or any information storage and retrieval system, without permission from the publisher.

Library of Congress Cataloging-in-Publication Data is available at loc.gov

ISBN 978-0-8077-5837-3 (paper)
ISBN 978-0-8077-7572-1 (ebook)

Printed on acid-free paper
Manufactured in the United States of America

24 23 22 21 20 19 18 17   8 7 6 5 4 3 2 1

Contents

Foreword *Philippa Campbell* ... ix

Introduction: What It Takes for Essential Outcomes ... 1
Bonnie Keilty

    Seven Concepts for Developing and Sustaining Positive Family–Professional Partnerships ... 4

    The Family–Professional Partnership as the Essential Relationship in Early Intervention ... 7

    Individualization as the Essential Ingredient of Family–Professional Partnerships ... 7

    Reflection as the Essential Component of Professional Growth and Development ... 8

    Organization of the Book ... 9

    About the Contributing Reflections ... 9

1. Ways of Knowing and Making Decisions ... 12
Bonnie Keilty

    Parenting Decisions and Cultural Lens ... 13

    Evidence-Based Practices ... 15

    Professional Reflection: Merging Evidence-Based Practices with the Family's Cultural Lens ... 19

    Lessons Learned: Ways of Knowing and Making Decisions ... 21

    Conclusion: Ways of Knowing and Making Decisions ... 26

    Questions for Daily Reflection ... 26

2. Family Priorities, Values, and Culture ... 27
Bonnie Keilty

    Parenting Within Family Priorities, Values, and Culture ... 27

	Partnering Within Family Priorities, Values, and Culture	29
	Family–Professional Reflection	30
	Lessons Learned: Family Priorities, Values, and Culture—Parenting and Partnership	34
	Conclusion: Family Priorities, Values, and Culture	37
	Questions for Daily Reflection	37
3.	**Family Engagement Dimensions and Practices**	**38**
	Hedi Levine and Bonnie Keilty	
	The Importance of Family Engagement	38
	Recognizing Engagement	39
	Ways to Promote Family Engagement in Early Intervention	40
	Paired Reflections and Lessons Learned: Development of Engagement	47
	Conclusion: Family Engagement Dimensions and Practices	51
	Questions for Daily Reflection	52
4.	**Family and Professional Power Players**	**53**
	Bonnie Keilty and Hedi Levine	
	Power in Partnerships	53
	Power of the Family	54
	Power of the Professional	58
	Sharing Power	60
	Professional Reflections: Valuing the Power of All Partners	61
	Family Reflections: Sharing Power for Empowerment	63
	Lessons Learned: Power Players	66
	Conclusion: Family and Professional Power Players	67
	Questions for Daily Reflection	68
5.	**Partnership Collaboration, Communication, and Confidence**	**69**
	Sagarika Kosaraju	
	Collaborative Decision Making in Early Intervention	69
	Preventing and Addressing Communication Misunderstandings	70
	Expressing Confidence	71
	Agreed-Upon Versus Recommended Decisions	72
	Family Reflection: Jen	74

Contents   vii

    Professional Reflection: Benny 76
    Lessons Learned: Partnership Collaboration, Communication,
        and Confidence 79
    Conclusion: An Intricate Dance 82
    Questions for Daily Reflection 82

6. The True Teaming Test 83
Bonnie Keilty

    Family as a Disciplinary Expert 84
    All of Us, Not Us and Them 87
    ... If Not Better 88
    Family Reflection: Teaming as Family 89
    Professional Reflection: Teaming with Different Families 90
    Lessons Learned: The True Teaming Test 93
    Conclusion: The True Teaming Test 97
    Questions for Daily Reflection 98

7. Going Deeper to Truly Understand 99
Bonnie Keilty

    Strengths-Based Interventions Through Families'
        Funds of Knowledge 99
    Going Deeper: Strategies Within Routine Activities 101
    Professional Reflection: Erin Discusses Going Deeper 105
    Family Reflections: Why Going Deeper Worked 107
    Lessons Learned: Going Deeper 108
    Conclusion: Going Deeper 113
    Questions for Daily Reflection 113

**Conclusion: Reflections and Lessons Learned on the
Unique Partnership Culture** 114
Bonnie Keilty

    Family–Professional Partnership as the Essential Relationship
        in Early Intervention 114
    Individualization as the Essential Ingredient of
        Family–Professional Partnerships 116
    Reflection as the Essential Component of Professional
        Growth and Development 117

    Systems Influencers   118
    The Privilege of Early Intervention Practice   119

Appendix A: Examples That Illustrate and Do Not Fully Illustrate Each Partnership Concept   121

Appendix B: Family-Professional Partnership Practices   125

Appendix C: Guiding Questions for Exploring Family and Professional Reflections   133

References   135

Index   149

About the Authors   158

Foreword

Effective early intervention (EI) services are rooted in compassionate and collaborative relationships among families and professionals. Developing and establishing these relationships may come naturally for some families and professionals, but in other instances, purposeful effort and skills may be needed to build and maintain the types of interactions that support families in raising their children with special needs. As pioneering special education researcher Ann Turnbull noted many years ago, family–professional partnerships are a journey undertaken by professionals and families together with an end goal of enhancing family and child outcomes as a result of participation in EI services. Sometimes this journey is easy and sometimes it is complicated by misunderstandings, miscommunication, or other challenges to establishing positive collaborations. Ann has reminded us always to engage in "empathetic reciprocity"—more simply put, to take the "shoes test" by asking and reflecting on the decisions made or actions taken by a family on behalf of their young child in light of the family's perspectives. Only when we "walk in another person's shoes" can we begin to understand or learn the perspectives of others.

As has been pointed out in many articles over the past 30 years, the quality of the partnerships between families and professionals influence the effectiveness of EI services in many ways. Yet professional preparation more often targets the interventions or strategies associated with each discipline and places less emphasis on teaching the skills needed to establish and build positive relationships with families. *Seven Essentials for Family–Professional Partnerships in Early Intervention* emphasizes that strategies and interventions are the *what* of supporting children's development and learning, but the family–professional partnership defines *how* those strategies may be integrated optimally into family life. Seven key concepts guide the family–professional process, provide insight for professionals about partnership building and their role in this process, and suggest that this is not always an easy process but one that may be implemented more easily when professionals are able to reflect on their beliefs, values, cultural perspective, and actions.

Culture has always been emphasized in family-centered approaches like early intervention, but it is increasingly important not only as more people of different backgrounds and cultures immigrate to the United States but as cultural assimilation has taken on less importance. EI providers may view families and what they believe families need through cultural lenses that are different from those held by a family, inadvertently creating a divide in the family–professional relationship that may impact negatively on the extent to which EI services benefit the child and family. As is illustrated in *Seven Essentials for Family–Professional Partnerships in Early Intervention,* professionals need to develop an understanding of their own cultural lens in order to be open to understanding and respecting each family's cultural beliefs and practices. Since so many aspects of EI are influenced by culture, understanding cultural influences on factors such as decisions, child rearing practices, or acceptability of certain interventions is a key to developing family–professional partnerships that work.

Get a group of EI providers together and you are likely to hear stories about the many challenges providers are facing when working with *some* families. More often than not, these challenges are related to something "gone wrong" in the professional's relationship with a family. *Seven Essentials for Family–Professional Partnerships in Early Intervention* outlines specific concepts that professionals may consider in reflecting on how to build partnerships with all families but especially with those whom the professional finds difficult. The reflections illustrating each of the concepts in action allow professionals to see themselves and likely identify with situations similar to those they have encountered. And the family reflections provide insight about family perspectives that professionals may not always be able to learn from the families with whom they are working. The reflective illustrations show valuable perspectives and possibilities for resolving situations that may guide the way for addressing real-life situations between families and professionals.

Theoretically, conceptually, and practically, early intervention has traditionally been centered on relationship-based interactions to support families and promote children's development, learning, and participation. The extent to which EI services actually result in positive relationships or developmental promotion has varied from family to family, provider to provider. That this book reflects on experiences and outlines components of a family–professional partnership should help professionals who are preparing to work in early intervention, as well as their more experienced counterparts, begin services for families and children with a goal of building a partnership based on the delineated concepts and maintaining the partnership via ongoing reflection. In this way, *Seven Essentials for Family–Professional Partnerships in Early Intervention* provides a valuable resource to help improve the outcomes of early intervention for all children and families.

—Philippa Campbell

Introduction

What It Takes for Essential Outcomes

Bonnie Keilty

It's not rocket science. This phrase is sometimes used when talking about early intervention support provision for families of infants and toddlers with developmental delays or disabilities. This statement suggests that early intervention (EI), and most particularly family–professional partnership (FPP), is easy. It suggests there is a prescription or a step-by-step plan for providing early intervention supports. In reality, early intervention is very complex work with multiple and always changing variables. To "do" early intervention well, this complexity, including the relationships within which the work occurs, must be embraced, understood, and planned for in every aspect of intervention practice.

So those who say "it's not rocket science" are only correct in the literal sense. Not only is early intervention sophisticated practice, but there *is* a science behind it: research that supports the nationally endorsed practices that guide the work. These practices come from the developmental science regarding child development in general, the development of children with disabilities, and the role families play in influencing child development. In *The Early Intervention Guidebook for Families and Professionals: Partnering for Success* (Keilty, 2016), EI research, practices, and expected outcomes were explored and illustrated, making the case for supporting families in their role as the primary promoters of their child's learning and development. More than 30 years of research shows that interventions are effective when they (1) provide families with strategies to foster their child's learning (e.g., Ketelaar, Vermeer, Helders, & Hart, 1998; Moore, Barton, & Chironis, 2014; Schertz, Baker, Hurwitz, & Benner, 2011; Shonkoff & Hauser-Cram, 1987); (2) assure quality parent–child interactions, attuned to the child's developmental characteristics and family culture (e.g., Innocenti, Roggman, & Cook, 2013; Kong & Carta, 2013; Mahoney, Boyce, Fewell, Spiker, & Wheeden, 1998; Raab, Dunst, Johnson, & Hamby, 2013; Trivette, Dunst, Simkus, & Hamby, 2013); and (3) encourage family confidence and competence in parenting their young child (Trivette, Dunst, & Hamby, 2010).

Families will have the strategies and resources to successfully meet their family and child outcomes when interventions focus on the multiple learning opportunities that occur in everyday family life and the family's effective use of responsive caregiving and specific engagement or "teaching" strategies tailored to the child's unique learning characteristics (Innocenti et al., 2013; Khetani, Cohn, Orsmond, Law, & Coster, 2013; Kong & Carta, 2013; Raab et al., 2013; Smyth, Spicer, & Morgese, 2014; Trivette et al., 2013). This research forms the foundation for nationally recommended early intervention/early childhood special education practices specific to family engagement. These practices were created by the Division for Early Childhood (DEC, 2014) of the Council for Exceptional Children and guide professionals to do the following:

- Share information so families can make informed decisions (F2)
- Collaboratively create plans with the family to identify the family's goals for their family and their child, and ways to meet those goals (F4), including the family's current, and potentially new, informal and formal resources available in their community (F7)
- Increase parenting knowledge and skills (F6) and inform the family about the value of the child learning all languages that comprise the child's home and community life (F8)
- Ensure families fully understand their rights (F9) and provide opportunities for families to learn advocacy and leadership skills (F10; pp. 9–10)

These professional practices are the *what* of partnering with families in early intervention. However, as Dunst (2000) identified years ago, "how help is provided matters as much, if not more, than what is done if positive [child and family outcomes] . . . are to be realized" (p. 100). This book furthers the work begun with *The Early Intervention Guidebook for Families and Professionals: Partnering for Success* (Keilty, 2016) by focusing on *how* EI professionals develop and sustain positive family–professional partnerships with each family.

Various models guide the *how* of early intervention, all designed to increase family confidence and competence in promoting their child's learning and development. These include the coaching model (Rush & Shelden, 2011) and family-systems interventions (Dunst & Trivette, 2009a; Dunst, Trivette, & Hamby, 2007; Trivette et al., 2010). The underlying expectations of these approaches are to build upon the family's already existing strengths and available resources according to how their family works and to develop new competencies based on the family's goals for their family and their child.

The family-systems intervention approach identified *relational practices*—professional beliefs, attitudes, and approaches that create a trusting, collaborative relationship to support family development—and *participatory practices*—professional behaviors that focus on meeting the family's goals. These practices are implemented in ways that encourage the family to fully engage in the goal-achievement process by making choices and decisions about the course of intervention (Dunst & Espe-Sherwindt, 2016; Dunst et al., 2007). Research has found that both sets of practices are necessary to maximize intervention effects. These practices directly affect parental sense of competence and overall well-being. These family characteristics, in turn, directly impact the quality of parent–child interactions and child development—the ultimate outcomes of early intervention (Trivette et al., 2010).

Relatedly, a review of early intervention research on coaching families found improved quality of life for families when coaching approaches used more relationship-based practices as opposed to interventionist-directed practices (Kemp & Turnbull, 2014). In other words, when interventions are provided through a relationship that results in families feeling empowered, positive family and child outcomes result. A few of DEC's Recommended Practices (2014) provide guidance on *how* to create and sustain these relationships. Professionals are expected to do the following:

- "Build trusting and respectful partnerships . . . through interactions that are sensitive and responsive to cultural, linguistic, and socioeconomic diversity" (F1)
- Be "responsive to the family's concerns, priorities, and changing life circumstances" (F3)
- "Recognize and build on family strengths and capacities" (F5)
- Promote family engagement " . . . in ways that are flexible, individualized, and tailored to the family's preferences" (F6; p. 9)

So, *how* early intervention supports families matters. And yet, emerging (i.e., preservice students) and practicing professionals can find it difficult to create and sustain relationship-based family–professional partnerships that promote parenting confidence and competence by building on existing strengths and addressing current needs (Amatea, Cholewa, & Mixon, 2012; Bronson, 2005; Fleming, Sawyer, & Campbell, 2011; Hebbeler & Gerlach-Downie, 2002; Jones-Harden, Denmark, & Saul, 2010; Keilty & Galvin, 2006; Roggman, Boyce, Cook, & Jump, 2001; Sewell, 2012). Part of this difficulty results from traditional EI perspectives and approaches centering more on the professional as leader–expert rather than guide–collaborator and attending to the child separate from, instead of embedded in, the parent–child relationship (James & Chard, 2010; Salisbury, Woods, & Copeland, 2010). Difficulty also arises from the inherent complexity described earlier.

Clearly, early intervention is sophisticated work, where each family–professional partnership is uniquely designed according to the family, child, and professional characteristics; family and parenting values and culture; and family priorities for EI. This requires deep understanding, analysis, and reflection of what is truly involved in positive FPPs. As R. A. McWilliam (2012) stated, "home visiting might be the most misunderstood and oversimplified issue in EI" (p. 227). This book is about digging deeper and looking closer at the complex and individualized work of FPPs and *how* to create and sustain this essential EI relationship.

SEVEN CONCEPTS FOR DEVELOPING AND SUSTAINING POSITIVE FAMILY-PROFESSIONAL PARTNERSHIPS

This book presents seven concepts of family–professional partnerships that have been drawn from research and practical literature, as well as clinical experiences, and aligned with nationally endorsed practices and capacity-building approaches. Each of the concepts briefly described below is discussed in a separate chapter of this book.

1. Differentiate Ways of Knowing and Professional Decisions. One of the complexities of EI work is distinguishing between what the evidence says is necessary for positive development and what our personal beliefs and priorities around infant–toddler development are. Because early intervention is embedded within the family's parenting approaches and everyday family life, the responses to these two distinct questions can be blurred. The personal beliefs of EI professionals might be swayed by the current evidence base, but are further grounded and understood within their own unique cultural lenses and beliefs about parenting and child development (Barrera, Kramer, & Macpherson, 2012). These ways of knowing are outside of EI work. There are multiple ways families may parent that are different, but no less effective, than how the EI professional does or would parent. Current and emerging professionals recognize their biases and perceptions around how best to parent and differentiate between the developmental evidence base and their personal biases.

2. Appreciate Family Priorities, Values, and Culture. Families purposely structure the way their family works to reflect their values, beliefs, and economic and social resources (Bernheimer & Keogh, 1995; Bernheimer & Weisner, 2007; Gallimore, Weisner, Kaufman, & Bernheimer, 1989; Keller & Kärtner, 2013; Maul & Singer, 2009). This is known as the family's individual cultural context. Families also organize their routine activities—what they do during the day and how they accomplish those activities—to meet the functional aspects of daily life and their goals for their entire family as well as each individual family member. The expectation is that these routine activities do not need to change; what families need are ways to meet their everyday priorities and larger family goals, given their child's unique developmental characteristics (Khetani et al., 2013). EI professionals work within each family's individual culture and routine activities, concentrating on that particular family's priorities and values for their child and family.

3. Build Family Engagement. A true family–professional partnership requires full and sustained family engagement in the EI process. Building family engagement is a developmental process that evolves over time (James & Chard, 2010). While professionals are used to entering into and creating FPPs, this experience can be quite new for many families. Some families may immediately join this partnership easily and fully, while other families will need more time to build a trusting relationship. EI professionals recognize what it means for the family to be truly engaged and intentionally use ways to support families in feeling more and more comfortable moving toward being a fully participating member of intervention.

4. Recognize the Power of Partnership Members. Both the family and the professional bring their own "power" to the FPP. EI professionals come with the power of being known as the expert (Spino, Dinnebeil, & McInerney, 2010). Families bring the power of being the most significant influencer of their child's learning, development, and sense of identity within the family culture and community. These powers can either be harnessed in ways that build family capacity or, intentional or not, diminish a family's sense of confidence and competence. EI professionals reflect on their perceptions and interactions to assure power is shared among partnership members. That way, the professional's power is used to bolster the family's power as a force for change toward child outcomes.

5. Openly and Honestly Collaborate and Communicate, and Demonstrate Confidence. While effective communication and collaboration techniques are necessary, successful interactions among FPP members reflect "build[ing] on each other's expertise and resources" (Turnbull, Turnbull, Erwin, Soodak, & Shogren, 2015, p. 161) through collaborative decision making. Professionals are proactive in anticipating and avoiding confusion, as well as reactively addressing misunderstandings when they still, inevitably, occur. Assessment and intervention outcomes are grounded in these effective collaboration practices (Bronson, 2005; R. A. McWilliam et al., 2011; Neisworth & Bagnato, 2004). The results of these collaborations are decisions that are truly *agreed upon* rather than *recommended* by the EI professional and *accepted* by the family. Agreed-upon strategies blend the family's expertise in their family, their child, and the way they parent, with the interventionist's expertise in child development, impact of disability, and developmental promotion strategies (Keilty, 2016; Keilty & Galvin, 2006).

6. View Each Partnership Member as an Equal Member of the Team. *Is the family truly treated the same as professional team members are treated . . . if not better?* This question is explored as a litmus test relative to whether the family is being viewed similarly as other team members. Professionals may—with the best of intentions and potentially unknowingly—exclude, overprotect, or make assumptions about families. These issues can be avoided by reflecting on families' perspectives before applying terms like "in denial" to describe families, coming to consensus when there are differing perspectives among family members and professionals, and sharing accurate and comprehensive information, opinions, and opportunities with families so they can make their own decisions for their child and family. The notion of "if not better" recognizes the powerful role of the family (see Chapter 4 for an exploration of power).

7. Dig Deeper to Truly Understand. Even with a strong partnership developed, there is the need for interventions to go deeper to ensure they truly fit the family. EI professionals talk about their struggles *getting* families to follow through with intervention strategies between home visits. If strategies and supports are really tailored to the family, professionals will not need to *get* families to do anything. Families simply will apply those strategies and supports because they are designed according to what the individual family already does and always expected to do as the parent. Essentially, families will obtain the knowledge, skills, and resources desired from EI, while at the same time applying their current competencies and resources to meet their family and child priorities (Dunst et al., 2007; Trivette et al., 2010). When going deeper, professionals further understand the particular family, with their particular child, at a particular point in that family's dynamic system. The challenge is to ask questions in a way that promotes reflection in the family's response without the family feeling tested, and then apply those responses in intervention design to assure a goodness of fit between the family and intervention (R. A. McWilliam et al., 2011).

These seven concepts provide a framework for EI professionals to reflect on their partnerships with families. They reveal the complexity and depth of each relationship. In analyzing these concepts, three themes arise for successful early intervention: (1) the family–professional partnership as the essential relationship in early intervention; (2) individualization as the essential ingredient of family–professional partnerships; and (3) reflection as the essential component of professional growth and development.

THE FAMILY-PROFESSIONAL PARTNERSHIP AS THE ESSENTIAL RELATIONSHIP IN EARLY INTERVENTION

Of course, the most important relationship for child learning and development is the one between the child and his or her family members, and the quality interactions occurring among them. However, the family–professional partnership has long been recognized as critical to early intervention success. This essential relationship is evident in all aspects of practical EI work—from eligibility determination to intervention planning and implementation to transitions. FPPs are also advocated for in administrative and professional development work where families have an equal voice in determining how systems are designed and educating current and emerging practicing professionals.

Based on the research described earlier, the goal of early intervention is to assure the family has the resources, strategies, and knowledge needed to promote their child's learning and development and meet their family's outcomes. A trusting, mutually beneficial, and open relationship increases the chances of meeting this aim (Trivette et al., 2010). However, this is easier said than done, as each FPP must be uniquely designed according to family, child, and professional characteristics, family and parenting values and culture, and family priorities for EI. To engage in such practices, current and emerging EI professionals understand, apply, and reflect on ways of partnering with families tailored to the diversity of families supported (Mahoney, Robinson, & Perales, 2004). Moreover, EI professionals find ways to ensure each family is readied for this kind of partnership. This book focuses on "how" early intervention is provided within the complex and individualized work of developing and sustaining a positive partnership with each unique family.

INDIVIDUALIZATION AS THE ESSENTIAL INGREDIENT OF FAMILY-PROFESSIONAL PARTNERSHIPS

Family–professional partnerships are challenging to create and sustain over time because each family is unique and each EI professional is unique. The way each partnership member influences the other is individual to that partnership. Each family may be at a different point in feeling comfortable with this type of relationship since an FPP is different from a relationship with a child's classroom teacher, clinic-based therapist, or doctor. Professionals nurture each relationship, gain trust, and prove to families that the EI partnership is worth their time and energy. The responsibility lies with the EI professional to create a partnership the family values and wants to be a part of. And yet, there are no cookie-cutter solutions. A professional who supports 20 families is engaged in 20 distinct relationships. No wonder EI professionals can struggle partnering with each individual family and, at times, feel overwhelmed! Yet, EI professionals understand the necessity of these partnerships for each and every child and family.

To be successful with each family requires individualization; the same approaches won't work with all families. *How* EI professionals partner with each family is going to be different. While engaged with this book, readers are encouraged to reflect on ways to individualize and differentiate their partnership with each family the same way they individualize and differentiate with each child.

REFLECTION AS THE ESSENTIAL COMPONENT OF PROFESSIONAL GROWTH AND DEVELOPMENT

Reflective, practicing professionals are doing just that—*practicing*. One aspect of practice is applying one's skills and expertise in the real world (i.e., *practice* as performing). Another is honing and enhancing one's competencies (i.e., *practice* as rehearsal). *Practice* involves continuous development—always learning. However, *doing* by itself does not result in learning; reflections about what one did and the result of those actions (i.e., practices) is what produces the learning. Reflection is an important component of growth and development in one's profession and has been found to be effective in acquiring new and enhanced knowledge and skills (Dunst & Trivette, 2009b; Dunst, Trivette, & Hamby, 2010; Nagro & Cornelius, 2013; Rush & Shelden, 2011).

Each family–professional partnership provides an opportunity for reflection, growth, and further mastery of one's practice. Reflection does not occur spontaneously. It is an active process of examination—questioning assumptions, practices, and biases and devising ways to accommodate new understandings in one's work (Etscheidt, Curran, & Sawyer, 2012; Taggart & Wilson, 2005). While each FPP is unique, generalized lessons learned can be constructed and applied to new partnerships, tailored to that unique family.

This book uses the authentic words, experiences, and perspectives of EI professionals and families to reflect on "what it takes" to build and sustain successful FPPs. These families and professionals "reflect productively" (Santagata & Angelici, 2010; p. 340) and model the reflective practices of "thinking aloud" (Taggart & Wilson, 2005, p. 10) about an objective situation, identifying their assumptions, and problem-solving potential alternatives (Etscheidt et al., 2012). Clarà (2014) defined *reflection* as "the thinking process that gives coherence to an initially incoherent and unclear situation" (p. 5). Readers are encouraged to reflect upon the families' and professionals' words, apply the lessons learned to their own work, and subsequently reflect on their use of those lessons as they engage with families as a way to illuminate what it means for effective family–professional partnerships.

ORGANIZATION OF THE BOOK

This book is organized around the seven partnership concepts. Each concept is described and illustrated in one chapter, which begins with an introduction to and definition of the partnership concept and resulting practices. Then, one family member supported by early intervention and one EI professional share their experiences in a family–professional partnership and reflect on how the particular partnership concept was demonstrated in practice. These reflections are then examined to identify a series of "lessons learned" that current and emerging EI professionals can use in their work with families.

Readers will walk away with a set of concrete practices to implement in their partnerships with families. These practices are provided throughout the chapters, signified with a dotted underline in the text and followed by the practice number in parentheses. The practices are also outlined in a collected list in Appendix B. Each chapter ends with "Questions for Daily Reflection" that EI professionals can use to reflect on their partnerships with families at the end of each day.

The final chapter, "Conclusions: Reflections and Lessons Learned on the Unique Partnership Culture," describes themes that result from and span the seven concepts, as well as systems needed to support successful FPPs. Additionally, the three themes of partnership, individualization, and reflection are revisited. The appendixes provide (a) an example and non-example of each FPP concept, (b) an outline of all the practices from each FPP concept, and (c) questions to guide one's exploration of the family and professional reflections. These tools are expected to support emerging and current EI professionals in planning, implementing, and evaluating the use of the FPP practices described.

ABOUT THE CONTRIBUTING REFLECTIONS

The families and EI professionals who contributed their reflections chose to convey them using the mechanism that worked best for the individual: in writing, via a phone conversation with Bonnie Keilty, or shared through their EI professional. In all modes, the reflections are the authentic words of the families and professionals. Any edits were made by the individual reflecting.

Each reflection illustrates how the focused family–professional partnership concept cannot be explained separately from the other FPP concepts.

Because the concepts are so intertwined, readers will see many of the concepts illustrated within each reflection. While the reflections are not concept specific, the lessons learned resulting from the reflections solely focus on the chapter's FPP concept. The following families and EI professionals contributed their reflections to this book:

Chapter 1: *Kurt Kondrich* is a dad, retired police officer, EI professional, and advocate who is passionately devoted to keeping policymakers focused on ABILITIES and investing early in our most precious natural resource—children!

Benton Johnson II is a clinical counselor and university professor who specializes in working with children and families in early intervention. He is the founder of Ephphatha Consulting Services which provides counseling services to Illinois individuals, families, couples, and groups. He enjoys teaching and doing presentations about effective interventions, working with persons in poverty, and play therapy approaches.

Chapter 2: *Marian Ghaly* is a mother of three children who shares how successful early intervention can be for the entire family.

Barbara Nieves is a speech–language pathologist who works with families within Connecticut's Birth to Three System.

Chapter 3: *Rashonda Harper* chose to contribute so that families will know that it is a benefit for their child, and also for themselves and their families, to learn about their children's needs, therapies, and the people that they work with—how much time and dedication, and care and love the professionals put into their work and the end results that are priceless.

Kat Bernardo is a practicing physical therapist whose primary love is playing with children all day long, therefore making the early intervention program the perfect fit.

Chapter 4: *Judith Najar* shares her family's story to show how family and professional investment creates the special bond of partnership to impact families and their young children. The authors appreciate her contribution in honor of Makai.

Cara DeLap has a bachelor's degree in rehabilitation from Stephen F. Austin State University and was an orientation and mobility specialist prior to becoming a developmental therapist.

Chapter 5: *Jen Wolsfeld* decided to contribute to this book because early intervention was life-changing for her family, and she thinks it is a shame that many parents are unaware that early intervention services even exist. Her family has seen success in leaps and bounds with the EI program. Her son was barely responding to his name when he started EI at 18 months, and now, 2 ½ years later, he is thriving in school and speaking in complete sentences! Jen truly believes that this success would not have been possible without the support her family received from early intervention.

Benny Delgado is a developmental therapist in Illinois and founder of Leaps & Bounds Family Services Inc., which was created so that families are able to receive services for their children in a manner that is respectful of their individual family culture, values, interests, and beliefs.

Chapter 6: *Michéle Pestel* is mom to her rainbow child Anya and staunch advocate for children, individuals, and their families who are affected by developmental, intellectual, and physical disabilities.

Jamie Mitchell has worked as a pediatric physical therapist since 2000 and has provided early intervention services in Hawaii since 2004. He is also the creator of *Help My Baby Learn* (HelpMyBabyLearn.com), a website dedicated to helping parents and caregivers learn about their baby's development and what they can do in order to help babies meet their developmental milestones.

Chapter 7: *Erin Campbell* is a pediatric occupational therapist in North Carolina who has served families in their homes, at schools, and in the clinic for the last 19 years.

The authors thank these contributors, as well as the families who shared valuable reflections and chose to remain anonymous.

These family and professional reflections demonstrate the complexity of building and sustaining effective family–professional partnerships, as well as the importance of reflection as an ongoing professional development tool. They illustrate how to apply the partnership concepts in targeted yet non-prescriptive ways, given unique family–professional contexts, and to reflect on that work to generate deeper thinking about those practices. Every one of the partnerships arose from the efforts of a thoughtful professional who worked hard to ensure a quality relationship with the family. Every one of them arose from a family striving to do the best for their child and family. The families and professionals contributed to this book in the expressed hope that readers could reflect—on families, infants and toddlers, intervention work, and what early intervention strives to be, namely, a support to families so that, in the end, parents get to be parents, children get to be children, and families get to be families—as they imagined they would—in their communities.

CHAPTER 1

Ways of Knowing and Making Decisions

Bonnie Keilty

There's a *New Yorker* cartoon where two mothers are face to face, each with an infant in a front baby carrier. One baby is facing outward while the other baby is facing toward the mother. The caption reads, "My baby is not on backwards—Your baby is on backwards" (Smaller, 1997). The reality is, assuming both children are well-positioned, neither mother is using the carrier "backwards." Both are using it the "right" way. The decision of which way to face the child was simply different. So it is with many decisions in early intervention (EI).

The family–professional partnership (FPP) has myriad decisions to make: decisions regarding what, where, and how to intervene. To make these decisions, the FPP identifies how best to promote child learning by blending EI professionals' knowledge and expertise of child development and evidence-based practices with the family's knowledge and expertise of their child, how their family functions, and their vision for their child and their role as parent. While this process might sound straightforward, the challenge lies in acknowledging and applying both ways of knowing—professionally acquired and culturally situated. The reason this is challenging is, just like any other individuals, EI professionals have their own perceptions of how best to parent. Of course, professionals' perspectives on parenting are informed by the evidence base. But the decisions EI professionals would make *as parents* are also further grounded and come to be understood within their own individual culture and beliefs. In the cartoon description above, one professional might lean toward the opinion of one mother, while another might lean more toward the other mother's. Since neither one is "right," the favored position most likely stems from the professional's own priorities as a parent versus a professional.

One of the many complexities of early intervention work is distinguishing what the evidence says is necessary for positive development from what EI professionals' personal beliefs and priorities are around promoting infant–toddler development. With each family and each intervention

Ways of Knowing and Making Decisions   13

opportunity, EI professionals continually examine their practices to determine whether they are interpreting the evidence base for the family or unintentionally overriding the family's parenting style with their own parenting beliefs and priorities. The purpose of this chapter is to explore these two ways of knowing so professionals can reflect on how their cultural lens informs their thinking in order to apply the evidence base to their EI work while contextualizing their personal parenting beliefs.

PARENTING DECISIONS AND CULTURAL LENS

Families make decisions about ways to parent that reflect their vision for their child's learning and development. These decisions are fundamentally linked to EI planning decisions:

- Ways are *strategies* used.
- Vision is *priorities*.
- Child learning and development are resulting *outcomes*.

For example, in the cartoon described above, perhaps the mother with the baby facing outward (*strategy*) wants to share the world she sees with her child (*family priority*). The baby can connect what is happening around her to the words the mother is using to describe those actions, as well as interact with people and objects along the way (*child outcomes*). The mother with the baby facing inward (*strategy*) might want her child to be connected to her and convey to him that they are "in this together" (*family priority*). The baby can regulate outside sounds and movement with the support of his mother and feel secure as the great wide world whirls around (*child outcomes*). EI professionals recognize the cultural lens they bring to strategies, priorities, and outcomes so that the decisions made by the family–professional partnership to promote child development fit the family's cultural lens (Ng, Tamis-LeMonda, Godfrey, Hunter, & Yoshikawa, 2012).

One's individual cultural lens is not comprised of a singular characteristic, such as ethnicity, but of numerous ones including socioeconomic status, acculturation, language, geography, and family structure that transact with the family's individual experiences, child characteristics, and influences of friends, family, and formal supports/education (Barrera et al., 2012; Friesen, Hanson, & Martin, 2015; Hanson & Espinosa, 2016; Hanson & Lynch, 2010; National Academies of Sciences, Engineering, and Medicine [National Academies], 2016). EI professionals can reflect on how their parenting beliefs changed during their professional education. These new beliefs may be different from those of their extended family who might, on the surface, be expected to have the same cultural lens as the EI professional, given similar cultural characteristics when considered broadly. Alternatively, EI professionals may see that, as parents, they do not follow everything they learned in school or recommend to families as professionals. Their role as *parent* is informed by more cultural influences than their role as professional. EI professionals can work within each *family's* cultural lens by implementing the following practices:

Know and apply the developmental research on cultural differences in parenting (1.1). While each family is unique, developmental science has identified some commonalities with regard to child development and parenting approaches among families with specific cultural characteristics. Families of different ethnicities vary as to when they expect children to acquire specific developmental milestones, such as particular gross motor and adaptive skills (Carlson & Harwood, 1999/2000; Friesen et al., 2015; Keller & Kärtner, 2013; Smyth et al., 2014; Spicer, 2010). These developmental expectations impact what strategies families use in order to specifically target those outcomes. EI professionals reflect on whether any differences in approaches between the EI professional and family are due to focusing on different outcomes (1.1.1).

Even when families are focused on the same outcome, the approaches used can differ. For example, when examining how families helped their child interact with objects, researchers found that the frequency with which mothers used verbal versus gestural and other nonverbal strategies or direct teaching versus facilitative approaches varied according to ethnicity (in this particular study, African-American, Dominican, and Mexican family backgrounds) and education level (Luo & Tamis-LeMonda, 2016; Tamis-LeMonda et al., 2012). The researchers concluded that, at least partially, these approaches were aligned with a larger cultural belief in how families help their children learn (e.g., guided teaching versus independent problem solving) and related family priorities or values being taught. EI professionals reflect on their own beliefs in how children learn as well as their larger priorities of what children should learn and then, for each family, determine whether any differences in approaches are due to these different beliefs and priorities even when focused on the same outcomes (1.1.2).

Know and apply the developmental research on universal approaches (1.2). Developmental science provides evidence of commonalities or universals—in both child outcomes and developmental strategies—that span cultural lenses. These commonalities are found in broader conceptualizations rather than specific outcomes or strategies. For example, Keller and Kärtner (2013) identified the universal child outcomes of belongingness, relating to others, and self-regulation. Universal parent–child interaction strategies common across cultures include attention, warmth, contingency, and responsiveness (National Academies, 2016; Keller & Kärtner, 2013; R. A. McWilliam,

2016). In the object-play studies referenced above, the researchers found that, even though strategies differed by culture, all families changed both the types of strategies used and the ways they expected their children to interact with different objects as their children developed and became more competent object interactors (Luo & Tamis-LeMonda, 2016; Tamis-LeMonda et al., 2012). In this example, the common strategy across ethnicities was scaffolding a just-right level of support. However, the particular child outcomes and family strategies used varied. EI professionals reflect on universal approaches to promote child learning and development; identify what those universals look like through their individual cultural lens and then, for each family, determine whether differences in approaches are alternate ways of meeting the same universals (strategies or outcomes) (1.2.1).

Utilize available resources to reflect on one's cultural lens and how it might impact one's interactions with families (1.3). There are multiple resources available for EI professionals to build and continue to enhance culturally responsive practices, including books, articles, and professional organizations (e.g., Barrera et al., 2012; DEC, 2010; Hanson & Lynch, 2010; Kalyanpur & Harry, 2012), as well as colleagues and reflective supervision that provide depth outside the scope of this chapter. By reflecting on and identifying one's cultural lens, EI professionals can acknowledge and avoid any biases toward a family's cultural lenses that may not adhere to the professional's perspectives. EI professionals reflect on their interactions with each family to identify ways they applied and could further enhance culturally responsive practices (1.3.1).

EI professionals who understand their own cultural lens can then apply early intervention's evidence base attuned toward an appreciation for the individual family's culture.

EVIDENCE-BASED PRACTICES

Evidence-based practices (EBPs) are the cornerstone of one's professional discipline (see Figure 1.1). Defined as "practices and programs shown by high-quality research to have meaningful effects on [child] outcomes" (Cook & Odom, 2013, p. 136), EBPs are utilized by EI professionals to maximize the effectiveness of their interventions. These practices distinguish what EI professionals provide from the type of advice families seek and obtain from family members, friends, colleagues, and neighbors. The advice given from these informal sources of support stems from their cultural lens. The advice EI professionals provide comes from the research that guides how to effectively implement EBPs, how to support families in effectively implementing those EBPs, and how the EBPs can be adapted to fit the family without losing their effectiveness.

Figure 1.1. Statements of Evidence-Based Practices by EI Professional Associations

American Occupational Therapy Association

"Occupational therapy is an evidence-based, science-driven profession that applies the most up-to-date research to service delivery." (www.aota.org/About-Occupational-Therapy/Professionals.aspx)

American Physical Therapy Association

"The physical therapy profession recognizes the use of evidence-based practice (EBP) as central to providing high-quality care and decreasing unwarranted variation in practice."(www.apta.org/EvidenceResearch)

American Speech–Language–Hearing Association

"It is the position of [ASHA] that audiologists and speech–language pathologists incorporate the principles of evidence-based practice in clinical decision making to provide high-quality clinical care." (www.asha.org/policy/PS2005-00221)

Council for Exceptional Children

"Special Education Professionals . . . identify and use evidence-based practices that are appropriate to their professional preparation and are most effective in meeting the individual needs of individuals with exceptionalities." (www.cec.sped.org/Standards/Professional-Policy-and-Positions#PROFESSIONAL%20STANDARDS,%20RIGHTS,%20AND%20RESPONSIBILITIES)

Effective implementation of evidence-based practices means that the practices are used with *fidelity*, that is, used the way the research "says" they should be implemented (Dunst, Trivette, & Raab, 2013; Reichow, 2016). Fidelity, however, does not necessarily mean that the EBP needs to be implemented in an overly structured manner or exactly the same way every time. What does need to be used in a particular way are the "active ingredients" that make the EBP effective (Abry, Hulleman, & Rimm-Kaufman, 2015; Harn, Parisi, & Stoolmiller, 2013; Lieberman-Betz, 2015). Active ingredients include particular components of the EBP, such as a specific strategy or order of strategies. However, it's not just the *use* of the active ingredients; it's the quality and the intensity (i.e., how often, how long) with which those active ingredients are applied (Abry et al., 2015; Harn et al., 2013; Lieberman-Betz, 2015).

EI professionals take care to assure the active ingredients are implemented as specified, but can add, modify, or eliminate other "ingredients," or components, that might actually make the EBP even more effective since it better fits the child or the family (Harn et al., 2013; Ledford & Wolery, 2013). For example, Brown and Woods (2016) found that evidence-based communication interventions did not need to be used only in play activities—the context in which the intervention research occurred. Instead, the specific intervention strategies (i.e., the active ingredients) could be used in families' other routine activities as they typically unfold. In other words, the context of the intervention could be modified so families could implement the interventions more frequently and naturally without losing the EBP's effectiveness. To implement the active ingredients of evidence-based interventions, EI professionals can implement the following practices:

Know and apply the evidence base for meeting specific child outcomes (1.4). National EI leaders, as well as the larger professional disciplinary fields (e.g., occupational therapy, physical therapy, special education, speech–language pathology), are increasingly identifying specific evidence-based practices and the active ingredients that comprise those practices. However, there are many practices where the current research still needs to be evaluated and other practices where additional research is required (Cook & Odom, 2013; Dunst & Trivette, 2009c). Despite these limitations, EI professionals do not abandon their professional role of working within the evidence base. There are practices where the evidence clearly shows ineffectiveness. These practices are avoided or discontinued. There are other practices that, while not fully supported yet, are situated in developmental theory and *informed* by some research, such as some of the recommended practices of one's professional discipline (National Academies, 2016; Odom, 2016; Reichow, Boyd, Barton, & Odom, 2016). EI professionals draw from what is currently known about a particular practice, which may not yet be deemed "evidence-based," and decide which practices to share with families and other team members (1.4.1).

In addition to the above limitations, no evidence-based practice will work for all children or all families (Cook & Cook, 2011; Cook & Odom, 2013). EBPs are also not "culture-free" and depend on the representation of various cultures within the research studies that deem the practice evidence-based (Busch-Rossnagel, 2005). As described earlier in this book, culture is defined through multiple characteristics, not solely race or ethnicity. There is a need for further guidance from research on which practices work for which families and children, given the complexity of factors that comprise each family system (Abry et al., 2015; Guralnick, 1997; R. A. McWilliam, 2015). Therefore, EI professionals continue to utilize individual child and family data to make decisions on the effectiveness of the EBP for the particular child and family.

EI professionals collect and analyze data on child progress toward meeting targeted outcomes and the fidelity to which the active ingredients of the particular interventions are implemented (McConnell & Rahn, 2016; Pretti-Frontczak, Bagnato, Macy, & Sexton, 2011; Reichow, 2016; Sandall, Schwartz, & Gauvreau, 2016). While collecting data on child progress is common EI practice, collecting and analyzing intervention fidelity may occur less frequently. In early intervention, of course, the family and other important adults in the child's life are the ones implementing the EBP. Therefore, fidelity to intervention occurs when families confidently and competently use those EBPs (Sutherland, McLeod, Conroy, & Cox, 2013). When families do not use an EBP, or do not use it with fidelity (as shown by the data), there may be a mismatch between the EBP and the family's everyday life—the context where the practice is expected to be used (Cook & Odom, 2013; Smith, Schmidt, Edelen-Smith, & Cook, 2013; Sutherland et al., 2013). For example, data demonstrating low family intervention fidelity suggests that the intervention is not aligned with family beliefs. When this occurs, the family–professional partnership can make one of the following decisions:

- Adapt intervention components that are *not* active ingredients (Harn et al., 2013; Ledford & Wolery, 2013).
- If active ingredients have not been determined from the research, modify intervention components that do not fit the family and collect child and family data to determine whether the certain ingredient is indeed active or unnecessary.
- Try a different EBP better suited to the family's cultural lens (Harn et al., 2013).

EI professionals use data-based decision making to determine child progress and how well the family implements the evidence-based practice (i.e., fidelity) to decide whether to continue or change the intervention (1.4.2).

Know and apply evidence-based practices for supporting family use of evidence-based practices (1.5). How well families implement specific EBPs is dependent on many factors. One is the goodness of fit of the practice to the family (Cook & Odom, 2013; Harn et al., 2013; Ledford & Wolery, 2013; Smith et al., 2013; Sutherland et al., 2013). Another is *how well* the EI professional supports, or coaches, the family in using that practice effectively (Dunst & Espe-Sherwindt, 2016; Dunst et al., 2013). The EI evidence base that identifies the active ingredients for coaching families (and others) continues to grow. For example, Dunst and Trivette (2009b) conducted a meta-analysis of the adult learning research to identify effective coaching strategies that result in an actual change in behavior as opposed to solely learning new knowledge that might not be acted upon. Rush and Shelden (2011) translated the coaching literature into specific implementation steps for EI professionals. EI professionals use these practices, with fidelity, so families can effectively learn and use development-promoting strategies with their children. Just like data are collected on the family's fidelity of using EBPs to support their child, data are collected and analyzed on how well (i.e., fidelity) the EI professional adheres to coaching EBPs to support the family. EI professionals use these data to modify coaching practices to best align with the evidence-based coaching practices. EI professionals draw from and apply with fidelity evidence-based practices that effectively support families as they obtain new ways to promote their child's learning and development (1.5.1).

Utilize available resources to develop an evidence-based practice toolbox (1.6). EI professionals are not alone in making decisions on whether specific practices are indeed evidence-based. Professional associations and other organizations, federal and state agencies, and researchers are creating research syntheses, practice briefs, implementation checklists, and other tools to facilitate EI professionals' knowledge and skills in identifying and implementing specific EBPs. At the same time, there is concern that the use of the term *evidence-based practices* is being overused and watered down (Cook & Cook, 2011). EI professionals need trusted sources for identifying actual EBPs. However, researchers evaluated 47 websites for special education professionals that describe specific practices as evidence-based (Test, Kemp-Inman, Diegelmann, Hitt, & Bethune, 2015). Results found that slightly less than half (43%) of those websites fell into the category of "do not trust." Therefore, EI professionals should avoid relying on the term *evidence-based* as the only indicator and look to sources that are known to be reliable and/or the actual evidence substantiating the evidence-based claim.

In addition to resources from a variety of online and print media, EI professionals can support each other in utilizing EBPs, such as sharing evidence-based resources, observing each other and providing feedback, and problem solving as a team. Through these mechanisms, EI professionals become knowledgeable and adopt various EBPs. EI professionals seek out resources that enhance their effective use of a variety of evidence-based practices that are shared with the FPP to inform EI decisions (1.6.1).

PROFESSIONAL REFLECTION: MERGING EVIDENCE-BASED PRACTICES WITH THE FAMILY'S CULTURAL LENS

Early intervention requires the melding of the two ways of knowing described in the previous section—the EI professional's knowledge of EBPs and the family's cultural lens. Benton, a mental health counselor supporting families in EI, reflects on how he has come to merge the two:

A family–professional partnership is a relationship that involves the intense investment of a professional, with extra-familial expertise, and a family, with intra-familial expertise, for the family's wellness and development. When reflecting on values regarding the family–professional partnership and teaming, I cannot forget about the importance of perspective. How I perceive me and the family impacts the outcomes of the mutual work we have to do. I, as a professional partner, am bringing my well-developed, guarded, and tested years of expertise. I molded this expertise in the venerated universities of the American education system, and it has helped develop my perspective. The fact that I have been called in to help, automatically puts me, as a professional partner, in a one-up position perspective. A one-up perspective is not necessarily the best place to be for two reasons. One reason is because one-up perspectives bring with them the overarching responsibility of creating the desired change in the family. The second reason is because it can demoralize the family. The one-up perspective can leave the family thinking and feeling lesser-than, which can lead to a communication shutdown. I realize that family communication with me is essential and absolutely necessary for me to join the family and help with change.

As a professional, I have a caveat. I must consider how to honor the family's years of expertise and balance that with the knowledge that the team is adding to this system. This is how we, or I, begin to think when working with families. Even stating the word *balance* seems to set up a polarization between the family and the professional team. This is the thinking that challenges us to change the way that we perceive the family in relationship to the team. So, I want to consider revising the statement to change the word from *balance* to *flow*. I must consider how to learn from the family's years of expertise and flow that with the applicable knowledge that the professional team is offering. While it may sound awkward, professional team members are really in flow with this family to the new place. After arrival to that place, we'll be discharged from the journey and the family will flow on with renewed confidence, trust, and skills.

Professionals have to be able to flow with the family's expertise. I have found that my knowledge has served me and other families well. While I have found this knowledge to work for me, when I join with a family, my knowledge may no longer work to serve their wellness and development well. It is just because I am a person with feelings that I may grieve the rejection of my expertise when I see that the family has other ways and means that are better suited for it. I am not a values- and judgment-free person, although I consistently seek to improve my acceptance and affirmation of other means that I do not hold as high. It is within the family–professional partnership that I have the challenge of identifying the family's ways and means instead of thinking that my rote and learned skills should be adopted by it. It is a different concept for me because I think that professionals, everywhere, normally do not take the time to think about their personal intense ways and means, and thereby inadvertently project, introject, and infuse their negative perspectives onto the family. This undermines the family–professional partnership and creates an adverse relationship. Sometimes I excelled, and at times I have missed opportunities.

A missed opportunity was when I took the perspective that my single-parented female-headed family wanted my explicit expertise. I, unknowingly, thought that she wanted a litany of well-researched discipline models to apply until she found one that worked with her family. So, in my mind, I had to immediately observe, find the family strengths, and see how this system worked so I could match the best discipline plan for the family. This might appear to be how this is supposed to work as a professional. However, along with the Occupational Therapist and Developmental Therapist, we were trying our logical, researched, and widely used ways and means, and were missing the whole point. We tried Conscious Discipline, sensory integration, speech and time-outs. All the sweat and toil that we were putting in was against the established flow of this family. This family had developed a flow of their own family management system that worked very well. It was tested, tried and true for many years. The family was happy with their overall structure. This family did not want a whole new system. The family really wanted help in identifying where their current structure could be strengthened. They also wanted to know how to best implement that strength. So, in short, it was a call for us to help them be their best family. This family could not be well with another structure.

During the trial of our methods, professionals would sometimes agree that this family was resistant to change. One professional was exasperated and said that she didn't know what else to do because this mother would not take any of her suggestions. The problem was not that the family would not take her suggestions, but that the suggestions were trying to suggest this family take away its identity. When we learned to learn the family first, we found that the family was only resistant to changing its identity. Once I learned the family identity, I could truly join the family and help the family detect the changes that they needed to make. My professional expert ways and means were not going to help the family. What helped the family was my ability to create the safe place for it to use their means, encourage them to try new ways, and help the family develop a healthy flow.

LESSONS LEARNED: WAYS OF KNOWING AND MAKING DECISIONS

Benton's contribution articulates the push-pull that can occur between evidence-based practices and the family's cultural lens or, as he calls it, the "family identity," when both are expected to be used in making EI decisions. Below, four lessons learned are described, drawn from Benton's contribution and related to the chapter purpose. Each lesson is illustrated using reflections from Kurt, the father in a family who participated in early intervention and later became an EI professional himself. [Note: Benton and Kurt are not from the same family–professional partnership; they share two different FPP experiences.]

Identify and Manage Professional's Own Emotional Needs to Focus on Meeting Early Intervention's Vision (1.7)

Consider the words Benton purposely used in his reflection: *guarded, tested, grieve*. These words describe, not one EI professional's (Benton's) *personal* cultural lens, but the whole professional teams' *professional* cultural lens. This lens might initially appear quite objective, with a focus on EBPs.

However, given the intimate, relationship-based nature of home visiting, EI professionals come to the family–professional partnership with emotional needs and might *grieve* when those needs are not met (Brotherson et al., 2010). The unmet emotional needs Benton described appear to come from a sense that the professionals' knowledge and expertise—their "personal, intense ways and means"—was not valued by the family. Brotherson and colleagues identified the importance of EI professionals getting their emotional needs met outside of the FPP, such as through reflective supervision and their personal resources. For example, through his own self-reflection, Benton found he could continue to use his expertise if he modified the nonessential elements of the interventions he brought to the FPP, keeping the active ingredients intact, to better "flow" with the family. In regard to his FPP, Kurt described the family "flow" in the following way:

> [The professionals are] the blockers and we [the family] are moving the ball forward with the ultimate goal of scoring a touchdown, which is the child graduating from EI with a strong foundation. [The professionals] are making the pathway so that we [the family] can keep moving forward.

Whether flowing or blocking, the EI professional joins alongside the family—with information, resources, and supports—to remove the barriers so families can meet their vision "with renewed confidence, trust, and skills" (Benton, above). Or, as Kurt described,

> When you have a child with a disability . . . it's like somebody turned the lights out. . . . You're kind of feeling around. If you're in a building and all the lights go out, it's really dark. . . . It's hard. If somebody shows up with a flashlight, like "Wow! Now I know where I'm going. Now I know which doorway to go through. I know how to get to my destination."

Share the Evidence Base Freely and Plainly (1.8)

Sometimes, EI professionals worry about sharing the evidence base with families when they know that the evidence base might be different from families' current thinking. They want to avoid what initially happened in Benton's reflection. However, just like professionals' personal cultural lenses most likely shifted by their professional education, families also revise their perspectives when new knowledge is acquired through various mechanisms (National Academies, 2016) such as the following:

- Observing and interacting with their own children (Ng et al., 2012)
- Observing others parenting
- Discussing with family, friends, and others

- Exploring websites, parenting books, articles, and mainstream media
- Discussing with specialists, such as EI professionals and pediatricians

This shift in thinking that occurred as a result of EI professional knowledge-sharing is illustrated in Kurt's reflection below:

> I can remember one of the therapists talking about early brain development. Things that I didn't really realize. . . . They helped me . . . understand . . . early brain development . . . what EI was. . . . [When I was growing up] there were no kids with disabilities in my community and my school. . . . It was all brand-new stuff so basically I was . . . learning back then about this stuff. I had changed my whole perceptions and beliefs.

This openness to change, while remaining within the family's individual culture, is why early intervention works, by enhancing families' knowledge about and interactions with their children. To do this, EI professionals translate the evidence base—as currently known—and other supporting knowledge, such as developmental theories and recommended practices, in ways that are understandable to the family and makes sense in the family culture. Note that sharing the evidence base means just that—offering information and potential strategies that are then discussed to determine the goodness of fit. In Benton's reflection, the barrier to this family–professional partnership appears to be that the EI professional team members were looking for the family to "take . . . suggestions" while missing the family collaboration part. Benton identified the need to "learn the family first" and "help the family detect the changes that they needed to make." Kurt described it this way:

> You have these babies and they're fragile and you're vulnerable as a family and, you know, there's all kinds of emotions. . . . So getting down to [the family's] level, whatever level that is, and meeting them there. . . . The only way you're going to move something forward is to first get to the level they're at and connect to that and then pull them forward. If you don't and you stay above them, talk down to them, whatever, shout out directions, then nothing is going to get accomplished.

And then there are times when families ask advice from EI professionals where there is no professionally guided response—a situation like that of the two mothers in the cartoon described at the start of this the chapter, where their decisions were simply different. In these situations, EI professionals become the same kinds of advice-givers as friends and neighbors. They acknowledge that their response is based on their personal cultural lens, and therefore not the only "right" way, and provide a rationale for their choice. With either a professional or personal lens, EI professionals collaborate with the family to weigh the pros and cons of different potential decisions to meet desired family priorities and expected outcomes (1.8.1).

Continually Verify That Interventions Are Meeting the Family's Priorities (1.9)

When the FPP is not working well, like Benton's originally wasn't, EI professionals can discuss with the family how the intervention is not fitting the family's individual cultural identity. From this discussion, the two partnership members can get back "on the same page." This disconnect can be prevented by starting with the family's priorities so interventions are designed from the beginning based on the family's individual culture. Kurt shares how the EI professionals considered his family's priorities of services and inclusion—in the community and within the family:

Community Service: The time when Chloe was born I was a policeman . . . [the EI team] knew our values were helping people, serving people. That was really a big part of who we were. Not just on the job but off the job. That, that's an important concept. [I'm] . . . really just basically doing the same thing now; just serving and protecting on a different level as an [EI] professional. . . . The EI team . . . provided us with LICC [local interagency coordinating council] information: when the meetings were, when there were meetings . . . for families and family fun activities. That's what really spurred me. I started going to a lot of those meetings. . . . It was their prompting of me to get involved, . . . I just wanted to learn more things about what was out in the community . . . and that's all been very positive. Chang[ing] my career . . . was a direct result of my EI team and the support and the prompting that they gave us as a family. . . . That was [EI] realizing early on that I was a community police officer; that's what I was. And then . . . taking advantage and connecting with things that they felt would be a good fit with me, which they did, obviously . . . bigger than ever. If they just came in there and done their thing and gone and they never recognized that, then . . . who knows what would have happened in life?

Community Inclusion: We told them early on that we like to go out. We go to restaurants, we go on trips. We love to go to the beach. . . . I didn't know anything about Down syndrome—what the implications were, what we need to do. . . . I didn't know all the possibilities of what this child could do, so we relayed to them . . . we want her to be part of this community, to do things, be involved in our church. . . . Chloe was born in May, and we had a beach trip planned for July. And we took her. Chloe was sitting on the sand in the Outer Banks in July, putting her feet in the water because they made us feel confident enough that we could take her to the beach.

Ways of Knowing and Making Decisions 25

Family Service: The EI professionals . . . really empowered [our son] to help his sister. . . . They got down to his level, a 4-year-old level, and realized his strength and his energy and his love and attention to his sister in a positive way to advance the goals in our IFSP [Individualized Family Service Plan]. . . . It's priceless. It really is. How siblings can be involved, or not, based on sibling and family interest.

Family Inclusion. Because we have such a big family in the area—we always had something going on on the weekend. We were booked solid . . . and I go back to EI and they really encouraged us to get out and . . . because we had so many family members and stuff around here to interact with them. Get her interacting with her cousins.

Kurt then identified how the EI professionals did not learn about these priorities solely by asking, but by observing:

I think you could just see from our house . . . almost like using police skills, investigative skills, looking around, seeing how our house is set up, what kinds of things we have laying around. . . . I think that's really important too. You could pick up a lot about a person—cultural and preference—by looking around.

Just like Benton had to "immediately observe, find the family strengths, and see how this system worked," the EI professionals supporting Kurt's family took the time to understand his family before deciding the best intervention approaches. And then, since families' perceptions and beliefs evolve, EI professionals continue to check in to make sure the chosen approaches still fit.

Fill the EI Professional Toolbox with a Variety of Evidence-Based Practices (1.10)

Even though the same intervention approach might work for two different children, their individual family cultures might require two distinct approaches. The same recommended approaches *not* used by the family in Benton's reflection might be valued and used by another family. Relatedly, Kurt acknowledged that having siblings learn intervention approaches may not be what every family values. He also confirmed the value his family found in a play group, but acknowledged that other families might not agree:

When Chloe was in EI, at 18 months, . . . [they] started this play group once a week . . . where families would come down there and meet and [the children] would play with their peers. That too really had a major impact on us because just to see her playing with other kids down there . . . they had like a little parent support type of thing and that was the other thing that they did early on was connect opportunities like that which . . . you know, not all parents wanted to go to it. It made a big impact on us. It was nice to share your fears, your concerns, and your experiences with other parents. Hey, guess what? There's somebody else out there going through this.

Therefore, EI professionals come to the partnership with multiple strategies, and ways to modify those strategies, to assure not only child-fit but also family-fit.

CONCLUSION: WAYS OF KNOWING AND MAKING DECISIONS

EI professionals are constantly distinguishing what they know from what they believe. It is the former for which families seek early intervention. Through reflection and questioning, EI professionals can continually strive to share their knowledge and expertise with families—knowledge that may uncover "better" ways of supporting their child's learning and development—while reinforcing families' individual culture.

QUESTIONS FOR DAILY REFLECTION

1. What were times my parenting cultural lens differed from a family's cultural lens? How did I approach this? What worked well and what could I enhance?
2. What strategies did the family and I agree the family would use between visits? How do I know those strategies are evidence based?
3. What were times a family asked for advice that didn't have an evidence base? How did I couch my response? What worked well and what could I enhance?
4. What strategies were modified to better fit the family? How did I know they would still be effective?
5. How did I collect data on my coaching fidelity? How will the FPP collect data on the family's fidelity of strategy use and child progress?

CHAPTER 2

Family Priorities, Values, and Culture

Bonnie Keilty

Chapter 1 illustrated how EI professionals recognize their *own* cultural lens, encompassing the multiple influences informing one's individual culture. Once recognized, EI professionals then differentiate and apply the early intervention evidence base within *each family's* culture. Families purposely design the way their family works to reflect their culture—their values, beliefs, and social and economic resources (Bernheimer & Keogh, 1995; Bernheimer & Weisner, 2007; Gallimore et al., 1989; Gauvain, 2013; Hanson & Espinosa, 2016; Keller & Kärtner, 2013; Maul & Singer, 2009). Respecting and working within the family's values and underlying culture, as individually defined, is a foundational expectation for EI practice (DEC, 2010; Hanson & Espinosa, 2016; Hanson & Lynch, 2010). This chapter will not repeat what has already been covered from other resources or provide the depth necessary to work from a culturally responsive perspective. Instead, this chapter describes how the family–professional partnership works within the family's style of parenting and partnering, and then explores those *responsive partnering* practices and subsequent lessons learned through the family–professional reflection.

PARENTING WITHIN FAMILY PRIORITIES, VALUES, AND CULTURE

Consider the different ways friends and extended family members parent: For example, some families have very structured routines where children are expected to go to sleep at a specific time and in a very specific way every night, and others have very flexible routines where children go to sleep at different times and places depending on what's going on with the family or according to the child's rhythms. Additionally, some families allow the child to pick out their clothes no matter how mismatched, and others choose the child's clothes so pants and shirts are well-coordinated. These are like the parenting decisions described in Chapter 1, decisions where one way is no better or worse than another, just different. Families decide what they want their child to learn (i.e., outcomes to be achieved) and how they choose to help them learn (i.e., strategies used) based on what's important to the family (i.e., family priorities). Families provide specific opportunities for their child to experience and learn, aligned to the developmental expectations of their culture, as well as to their cultural traditions and ways of being (Bronfenbrenner, 1979, 1993; Dunst, Raab, Trivette, & Swanson, 2010; Guralnick, 2011; Institute of Medicine, 2000). Those learning opportunities occur through the family's everyday routine activities—what the family usually does with their child throughout the day and over the week. When early intervention enters the family's life, EI professionals and families form a partnership to understand and work within a family's routine activites and cultural expectations by doing the following:

Intervene within the family's routine activities, attuned to the family's individual culture (2.1). As stated previously, the way routine activities usually occur reflects the family's individual culture, values, and priorities. Therefore, EI professionals do not only identify and use the family's routine activities; they also examine how those routine activities occur within the particular family including

- structure or flexibility of the routine activity;
- materials used;
- when the routine activities occur; and
- the people involved in the routine activities.

The more the routine activities can remain unchanged, except for modifications to support child learning (i.e., active ingredients), the more the routine activities will continue to reflect the family's culture and parenting priorities and style. When modifications do occur to any characteristics of the routine activity, the family–professional partnership makes sure that these changes continue to reflect the family's way of being (i.e., individual culture).

Support the family in parenting the way they want to parent (2.2). All families help their children learn—to move, interact, play, and participate in everyday life. Research has found that families identify and utilize development-promoting strategies aligned to their individual cultural expectations and desired outcomes as well as their child's unique developmental characteristics (Bernheimer & Keogh, 1995; Bornstein, 2002; Diamond & Kontos, 2004; Gallimore, Weisner, Bernheimer, Guthrie, & Nihira, 1993; Gallimore et al., 1989; Hanson & Espinosa, 2016; Keilty & Galvin, 2006; Kellegrew, 2000; Khetani et al., 2013; Maul & Singer, 2009; Institute of Medicine, 2000; Pierce, 2000; Turnbull, Blue-Banning, Turbiville, & Park, 1999). It's a natural part of the parenting process for families to facilitate their child's learning and development in their own way. This doesn't change just because their child has a developmental delay or disability. Therefore,

Family Priorities, Values, and Culture

EI professionals work within the family's vision of parenting—their priorities, outcomes, and strategies (Hanson & Espinosa, 2016). EI professionals *come to understand* the individual family's parenting vision, *relate* any developmental recommendations (e.g., outcomes, strategies) to that vision, and then *confirm* with the family whether or not the recommendations actually fit the family's vision. The FPP can then be confident they are working the way the family wants to parent.

PARTNERING WITHIN FAMILY PRIORITIES, VALUES, AND CULTURE

EI professionals assure that interventions are designed so that the interactions between family members and their children occur as the family envisioned they would. Equally essential to successful early intervention are the interactions between EI professionals and family members. The first family DEC recommended practice (DEC, 2014) summarizes this expectation: "Practitioners build trusting and respectful partnerships with the family through interactions that are sensitive and responsive to cultural, linguistic, and socio-economic diversity" (p. 8).

Responsiveness requires an openness to understanding each individual family's partnership style and then providing supports in that manner. This increases the family's comfort in partnering and builds trust that the partnership is created to strengthen, rather than judge or change, the family. For example, Al Khateeb and colleagues (Al Khateeb, Al Hadidi, & Al Khatib, 2015) identified that many Arab-American families use more nuanced, nonverbal communication to convey their perspectives—most particularly before a trusting relationship is established—as well as rely on their extended family to contribute to decision making. If an EI professional is working with a family who holds these perspectives—depending on multiple family factors in addition to ethnicity (see Chapter 1)—the EI professional could (1) attune to the family's more subtle communications and then confirm whether or not she is reading the family accurately and (2) make sure there is time for the family to gather other family members' opinions before decisions are made. The latter practice might mean shifting timelines or procedures to accommodate. For example, after a family–professional partnership "agrees" on an intervention strategy, the agreement is considered tentative until the family member can confer with other family members. The EI professional might check in with the family before the next visit to learn the verdict. If the family chooses not to use the strategy, the EI professional might visit sooner than scheduled to identify an alternative strategy. Therefore, EI professionals develop comfort and competence in purposefully seeking to understand each family's partnership style, interacting and working accordingly, and eliciting feedback to assure the professional's interactions are indeed responsive to that partnership style (2.3) (Hanson & Lynch, 2010).

Essentially, EI professionals alter their interaction style and expectations of what each partnership would look like based on the family's interactions and expectations (Hanson & Espinoza, 2016). These include the following:

- Communication approaches
- Level of formality in partnering with professionals
- Kinds of supports expected
- Roles of each family member in decision making and childrearing

For example, an EI professional might be quite used to creating very informal relationships with families where casual conversations of current events and goings-on are discussed. While this might work for some families, others might want their relationship to be friendly, but more formal, focused solely on intervention topics. Or, in back-to-back visits, an EI professional might partner with one family who is boisterous and talks really fast, and then a second family who is quiet and talks slowly and methodically. Just like adults use responsive caregiving approaches to adjust to a child's interaction style, EI professionals are flexible in how they interact and partner with each family according to the family's pacing, rhythms, expectations, and approach to partnership. This *responsive partnering* approach to meeting the family's parenting and partnership style is illustrated below in the family–professional reflection.

FAMILY–PROFESSIONAL REFLECTION

The family–professional partnership of Marian, the mother of a family receiving EI supports, and Barbara, a speech–language pathologist, shared a speaker phone as they reflected together. What is not well represented in the written transcript is the unmistakable partnership demonstrated. When either Marian or Barbara was speaking, the other partner could be heard jumping in to further reinforce the points being made.

Marian: In the beginning, actually when [the EI professionals] . . . explained the program to me, they explained that it was a coaching method, which means they will stay with me for an hour or 2 hours during the week. But then they show me what to do and then I need to follow up on it and use it in everyday life. It's the best part of the program because . . . one hour a week—which I agree—is not enough for him to accomplish. . . . Actually let me tell you what they do. They come in—Barbara comes twice a month, [the primary EI professional] comes . . . once a week. . . . The session is around an hour and we sit down . . . and then they show me what I should do. . . . What I like about it is . . . I actually can use it in everyday life because they come to the house. I still go to the school [with Anthony] and once

Family Priorities, Values, and Culture 31

a week they offer a program there. But then in my house, in my regular routine, I can use it every single day.

[The EI professionals came to understand the family's routines because] well, they asked. Every day when everybody comes, we make a progress note [of] what to work on next time. They tell me, "What's my main problem? What's my main concern?" and depending on what that is . . . we make our plan [for next time]. . . . So it changes sometimes accordingly. They're very flexible also.

Barbara: Well, I think that we are primarily listening to Marian's needs and building a relationship with her. When we initially met with her, . . . [we asked] what parts of her day were hard? What parts of her day were easier? What would she like to see go better? Then we reviewed those activities, taking into account her priority on what areas of her son's development she would like to address. Anthony's communication was one area of development that impacted her day. . . . We talked about how she and Anthony could communicate better. But we focused on his communication within her daily routines which she really had trouble with. [For example] bath-time and going outside. We just came back from a walk [because] she was not taking him outside. Also how to play more appropriately with his sister. . . . Within those activities we addressed her priorities and Anthony's needs.

Marian is saying that we're telling her what to do, but we're really talking about it—What worked? What did you try? What may be another alternative to try if that's not working? Sometimes we are sharing some information we know about young children. We are asking questions, trying strategies and seeing what worked best for her. So it makes sense that there is this constant communication between Marian and ourselves. I think [it] is really a partnership that's working.

[The EI professionals came to understand the family's routines by] using our initial Individual Family Service Plan. We're really talking to her about the daily routines—what's going well and what's not going well. Then, as our visits began to progress, we discovered some additional avenues that [Marian] may not have thought of that would be beneficial. . . . For instance, one of the initial activities I believe was play—and how to have him play and communicate better . . . then outside play [was added] . . . because she really hasn't done that. So we've taken play and expanded it to a different play activity. Or, bath-time. How do we expand that? [Marian] felt that she couldn't bathe him by herself. When we did that experience, we also moved to other opportunities for learning and interacting within the bath-time activity. Whether it be the [initial focus on] play or helping him to undress and get dressed. I think, it's these open-ended questions—"How are things going? What are your feelings? What have you tried? What else can we try?"—that we really discovered different opportunities for learning and success in the different family activities.

[Learning about the family's routine activities unfolds over time by] . . . really revisiting the daily activities. . . . Much of our conversations are about trying new things and . . . how to help Marian help Anthony reach the next level in his development.

Marian: I just want to add that . . . they're not telling me what to do. They're asking me to see things or to figure out things by myself. . . . I realized, you know what, that actually this was better [than telling me] because . . . Barbara makes me draw my own conclusions . . . and I think she also started to give me confidence. . . . She's trying to tell me, "You know what? You can do it! You know how to do it. You need a little bit of help. You don't need that much help, but you do need help." I like that sometimes when we were sitting down and I do something, I am looking for her to correct me but she doesn't. . . . And at the end of the visit I ask her, "Barbara, is there anything different . . . can I do anything different?" and she says, "What do you think we can do?" and . . . [after I tell her my ideas, she says] "Yes, that's correct. Exactly. That's what you should do." . . . I [also] think the notes . . . at the end of the visit—they write what they did during the visit and . . . what they're going to do next week. Sometimes I tell them, "Okay, what can I work on with [him] this week?" So she tells me, "What do you think?" . . . So I said, "Okay . . . I'm going to have him play and . . . to extend his attention span." . . . I think also that you have to account for what you did; not really homework or anything but it's good that you have somebody to work with you.

[At the next visit] . . . we sit down and chat . . . and I tell her, "You know what? I went to the park yesterday and he threw a tantrum at the park and I didn't know what to do and this is what I ended up doing . . . should I have left him or what should I have done?" . . . In the beginning [of EI], it was more, "What should I do? What should I do?" but now it's more I take their advice or their opinion or I think I'm much more comfortable that I'm not going to be judged. You know what, it's all a learning process and we're all trying to do this for him.

Barbara: [When Marian wasn't able to fit certain strategies into her day or the strategies didn't quite work within her day] . . . we [would] have some discussions as to why something might not have happened. . . . I think it's good to, again, know why these things did not happen and how to make it happen. Or, to know if it is still a priority to make it happen. I always feel like I want to know the reason the parent did not try a strategy. Is it still a priority? Or how can we make it happen? So I think it is important to have a follow-up discussion. . . . What's the frequency [of my visits]? Again, I am not the primary person for Marian. I am the support person. So I don't think the frequency of my visits impacts follow-up discussions. It is important to have those discussions. The primary provider will follow up on those discussions.

Family Priorities, Values, and Culture

... I'm always with the primary [EI professional] during my visits.... It would be very rare that I would make a separate visit. I also want to hear the teacher's concerns and if there's something she feels that she needs my help with. I'm really there to support [the primary professional] and Marian, of course. And we also have those opportunities outside of our visits when we do our teaming. Within our staff meetings we review what [the primary professional's] next steps would be and questions she might have for myself or other team members ... so everyone really is on the same page.... We all use the same strategies.

Marian: [At the beginning of early intervention] ... I felt that Barbara only comes twice a month and I felt like that wasn't enough for Anthony. So I put him in private speech classes 2 months ago and that was only once a week ... they go for an hour and 25 minutes. So I actually appreciated the [EI] program more when I left [the speech class]. I appreciated the program more when I saw what the other programs did because the other program, [he] only goes once a week. They don't know him as well.... I think [EI is] much less formal for him. When he sees [the primary EI professional]—he's in the street or something—he can go say "hi" to her now because he is very comfortable with her. Not ... only in the school setting or in traditional settings but she sits with him ... you can see with Barbara. It's not like, "Now it's time for school," or "Now it's time for education." So they come, they play with him at home and being in the home setting I think he feels they're more like family ... not they're here for a specific task and then they're going to leave. I think, in the beginning ... I was very skeptical about the program to be honest. But then I asked a couple of friends and they highly recommended the program, and ... I guess because of their reference, I really like the program. I think it works great.

... I also have to think of new things to do in the house. I have to use the resources that I have and just do new things with it.... I have two older girls, so I look at them and like, "Okay, this is a playhouse." I never thought to think of a playhouse for the boy, but you know what? I took it out and he's actually playing with it! ... We went outside today and I ... figured ... he can use the chalk to draw on the asphalt on the driveway. You know, I think that sometimes we have to think outside the box. But then you have to think, what's right in front of your eyes? And unless somebody tells you, [you might not see it].... For example, the high chair. I only used it as a high chair.... One time [the primary EI professional] was here and Anthony wants to sit with us at the table ... [and the primary EI professional said] "Why don't you move the table or the whole thing in front of the high chair, lower it down, and then push it to the table?" So now he's actually sitting on the high chair while at the same time he's sitting with us at the table! I think things like that. Sometimes it's right in front of your eyes ... and you don't really see it so ... it helps you think outside the box. They don't give you the solution ... otherwise

I would be . . . calling them every two seconds, "What should I do? What should I do?" They give you more confidence in yourself. . . .

Barbara: I feel satisfied when [Marian] says, "I can think of things and I am confident." And not only with play activities, but in all of her other daily activities that she may not have mentioned—snack-time, going outside—and that wonderful experience with bath-time. Now that routine is successful for Marian. I've seen changes in the months that we've worked together—where before there may have been a little bit more probing [from me] about what other opportunities are there—whether it be for helping her problem-solve or use strategies for communication . . . she is now able to think—taking the initiative. This is where we've met with success in our interactions together.

Marian: There's struggles every day and everything. But I think now . . . we went to a play group a couple of weeks ago and there was the mom . . . the toddler was running from the mom and she was apologizing to everybody like, "I'm so sorry. I'm so sorry. I'm so sorry." And I'm like, "No, it's fine." Anthony was running just last week, so I said, "You know what, I mean, been there, done that." . . . Sometimes your [children] are the only ones running . . . [Anthony] was running. Now he's one of the first ones to sit down and listen and participate.

LESSONS LEARNED: FAMILY PRIORITIES, VALUES, AND CULTURE—PARENTING AND PARTNERSHIP

The success that Marian and Barbara described resulted, in part, from the responsive partnership practices described in this chapter. The family–professional partnership intervened within the family's authentic routine activities—taking a bath; eating a snack; and playing alone, with Marian, and with Anthony's sister. The FPP added playing outside and going for walks as new routine activities. Since it was Marian who identified these routine activities, the FPP was assured they were meaningful times for early intervention. The professionals were attuned to the importance of how the routine activities usually occurred. They changed the times of their visits so interventions happened when the routine activity usually happened. The high chair was an example of using the same materials the family usually used and then simply modifying *how* the chair was used in order to meet the parenting goal of Anthony sitting at the table. Marian confirmed that early intervention worked to "use the resources that I have and just do new things with it." Barbara affirmed that the ultimate goal was to avoid changing the family's routine activities and, instead, "give more depth to the different family activities" to further help Anthony learn.

The success of the FPP suggests that it was aligned with the family's partnership style. For example, Marian felt comfortable initiating questions (e.g., "Can I do anything different?"). Other families may not take that initiative, thinking that they should not question professionals. At those times, responsive professionals can frequently invite questions and, if none arise, share some potential questions (e.g., "Sometimes, families wonder . . . "). This responsive partnering approach is further illustrated in the first lesson learned below.

Effectively apply the active ingredients for coaching families, blended into the family's style of parenting and partnering (2.4). Barbara and Marian's partnership illustrate how EI professionals can both know and apply the evidence-based practices for supporting family strategy use (see Chapter 1) *and* provide responsive partnering. Right from the start, the EI professionals explained to Marian how early intervention worked and why. This set the stage for the FPP to utilize evidence-based coaching practices. While at first Marian was skeptical of the coaching approach, as Barbara and the other team members provided supports in this way, Marian began to see the benefits. While this change in perspective was supported by her friends' endorsement of the EI program and her experience with a private speech class, this shift would not have occurred if the EI professionals abandoned the coaching practices in response to Marian's expectations that early intervention would provide specific recommendations (e.g., "What should I do?"). Instead, the EI professionals used coaching, but adapted it to initially provide "a little more probing" and more direct "wondering" of potential strategies (e.g., "Why don't you move the table . . . in front of the high chair . . . ?"). As Marian further understood how coaching worked, the EI professionals scaffolded their approach so Marian could begin to "see things and figure out things by myself" and "draw my own conclusions." As Marian saw that she was not being judged, this way of working not only felt comfortable, but became "the best part of the program."

Encourage the family to share their thoughts and ideas first before giving the professional's perspective (2.5). Barbara and the other professional team members asked Marian about the routine activities that mattered to her, the strategies Marian tried, and what strategies she thought could be potential alternatives. There are three reasons to encourage the family to speak first (Kalyanpur & Harry, 2012; P. J. McWilliam, 2010).

First, the EI professional learns more about the family's individual culture—how the family thinks about parenting. With this knowledge, professionals can respond specifically within that lens. For example, when Anthony exhibited challenging behaviors in the park, Marian wondered if she should have left him alone rather than respond. By knowing what strategies Marian was considering, the FPP could discuss the potential options, weighing the pros and cons of each.

The second reason to encourage the family to speak first is that any strategies the family identifies will already be attuned to their cultural lens. For example, some families might not ever be comfortable with a boy playing with a playhouse. EI professionals might have helped Marian "think outside the box," but she identified and tried this idea herself, which meant she was comfortable with the strategy features.

And finally, when families arrive at ideas themselves, confidence in their abilities builds. Families may defer to professionals when professionals share their ideas first, thinking they are the experts (see Chapter 4; P. J. McWilliam, 2010). When families share first, professionals can reinforce the families' ideas by confirming their effectiveness or individual appropriateness and/or building off those ideas to become even more effective. It is important to note that the conversation *starts* with the family's ideas. EI professionals contribute their perspectives to help decide the best course of action.

Use "constant communication" to assess and revisit any decisions made (2.6). The family–professional partnership of Marian, Barbara, and the primary EI professional continually discussed how well early intervention was fitting within the family's life. When strategies didn't fit, the FPP explored why: Was the outcome no longer a priority? Were the supports provided the right ones (e.g., frequency)? Were there new, more pressing priorities? The need for this conversation is pretty clear when families are not implementing the agreed-upon strategies. However, this conversation is equally important when families are using the strategies. Families may think that they *need* to use the agreed-upon strategies, even if they don't fit their parenting vision. They might think the strategies are the only ones that could work. Or, they might think, since they agreed with the strategies, they cannot change their mind. It is up to the EI professionals to continually check in and explicitly ask about the family's feelings on the strategies: Did they expect to use these kinds of strategies as a parent? What parts fit their parenting expectations (if any)? What parts don't fit (if any)? With this information, the FPP can brainstorm ways to adapt or replace any strategies that do not fit well. By openly asking for feedback, the FPP avoids assuming that the way early intervention is currently occurring works for the family.

Apply responsive partnering regardless of role (2.7). Barbara is not the primary service provider for Marian's family (Rush & Shelden, 2011). She co-visits with the primary EI professional and sees the family less frequently. However, this "secondary" role did not stop her from developing a responsive, close relationship with Marian's family. Barbara knows the family's priorities, desired outcomes, and routine activities. Barbara knows how

Family Priorities, Values, and Culture

best to partner with Marian. The teaming among EI professionals that occurs outside of intervention visits most likely facilitated this understanding. However, Barbara then applied this knowledge to create a responsive relationship with Marian's family.

CONCLUSION: FAMILY PRIORITIES, VALUES, AND CULTURE

When EI professionals are responsive to the individual family's priorities, values, and culture, the family–professional partnership works in ways that feel comfortable for families. This comfort results from interventions fitting within the family's vision of parenting. Basically, it's about assuring that the FPP is meeting the overarching expectation for early intervention that was shared at the end of the Introduction:

> Parents get to be parents
> Children get to be children
> Families get to be families
> As they imagined they would . . . in their communities.

QUESTIONS FOR DAILY REFLECTION

1. How have I assured that the priorities, outcomes, and strategies addressed during the visit fit the family's individual parenting vision, values, and culture? What else could I have done?
2. How have I assured that the way I partnered with each family fits the way the family feels most comfortable partnering? What else could I have done?
3. How well did I gather the family's thoughts and ideas first, and then respond based on their statements? How could I enhance that practice?
4. How did I contribute to the family's evolving parenting understanding and approach, without sacrificing their parenting vision? What could I do differently next time?

CHAPTER 3

Family Engagement Dimensions and Practices

Hedi Levine and Bonnie Keilty

Engagement is a state that may be hard to describe; but it is easy to recognize when the elements come together. *Engagement* means connection, indicating a trust and investment in the early intervention process. Engagement is demonstrated by interest, initiation, and active participation (Peterson, Luze, Eshbaugh, Jeon, & Ross Kantz, 2007). Family engagement is a critical component for successful early intervention and, more specifically, the family–professional partnership (Kingsley & Mailloux, 2013; Moore et al., 2014; Schertz et al., 2011). Just like children need to be engaged for learning to occur, families need to be engaged for the FPP to work. In this instance then, family engagement is different from what happens after families are engaged, when the practices typically defined as "coaching" or "consultation" are used to enhance the family's capacity to meet their child and family outcomes. Therefore, EI professionals identify opportunities to promote and sustain family engagement as a prerequisite for productive FPPs focused on promoting child learning and development. This chapter explores the attitudes and interpersonal skills used to engage with families, the various dimensions of engagement, and ways to advance engagement with each individual FPP.

THE IMPORTANCE OF FAMILY ENGAGEMENT

When engagement "works," both family and professional partners are actively involved in meeting FPP goals. This quality of mutual involvement is similar to gears turning together to make something move. The two gears that comprise FPPs are the family and the EI professional. The FPP gears turn in synchrony to move the third gear, the child, which creates the triadic relationship used to achieve EI goals (Brown & Woods, 2016; Campbell & Sawyer, 2007; McCollum & Yates, 1994). An analysis of an Early Head Start program found that parent engagement, in addition to home visiting quality, was related to home visitors' ratings of "family improvement" (Roggman et al., 2001). Family engagement in EI visits focused on promoting child learning and development was found to have positive effects on both child and family outcomes (Kingsley & Mailloux, 2013; Moore et al., 2014; Schertz et al., 2011).

Center-based early childhood programs strive for family engagement to maximize child outcomes. Research has found families' level of engagement in center-based programs differed based on multiple family factors, needs, and interests (James & Chard, 2010; McWayne, Melzi, Schick, Kennedy, & Mundt, 2013). Unlike center-based programs, however, early intervention *depends* on family engagement since the family is the primary implementer of intervention. When EI professionals *engage* families in intervention visits, families, in turn, become increasingly effective in promoting their child's learning and development between visits, enhancing family confidence and competence (Dunst et al., 2007; R. A. McWilliam, 2000, 2010a, 2016; Trivette et al., 2010). Therefore, family engagement is not the goal itself, but a fundamental element to family–professional functioning.

RECOGNIZING ENGAGEMENT

What does it mean for families to be engaged in early intervention? Drawn from their research of the Parents as Teachers home visiting program, Wagner and colleagues (Wagner, Spiker, Linn, Gerlach-Downie, & Hernandez, 2003) identified various dimensions of family engagement, organized by increasing levels of buy-in and participation. Below, these dimensions are described and extended to illustrate what they might look like in early intervention.

- **Present and available.** This level occurs when families enroll in early intervention and continue with intervention visits. During those visits, families engage by staying nearby the intervention (i.e., present), passively observing, and potentially waiting to be invited to participate.
- **Involved.** At this level, families participate in intervention visits by attending, engaging in conversations, seeking advice, and perhaps helping the professional maintain child attention and engagement. EI professionals still take the lead but families are actively, as opposed to passively, participating.
- **Applying supports provided.** At this level, families participate by actively discussing information shared and trying out strategies generated by the EI professional. Families also use the professional-led information and strategies between visits.

- **Generalizing supports.** This highest level of family engagement occurs when families integrate the information and strategies from the visit and, in collaboration or on their own, apply the information and strategies to different routine activities, to new child competencies or concerns that arise, or to additional, substitute, or modified strategies and resources that best fit the individual family.

Upon further examination of these dimensions, three important points arise for EI practice. The first is to acknowledge that family presence and availability are, in fact, dimensions of engagement. Without this recognition, EI professionals might assume that the family is not interested in participating and may not work to build engagement. But acknowledging that the family *is*, in fact, engaged gives EI professionals a "starting point" from which to build higher levels of engagement. This leads to the second point, namely, "get[ting] your foot in the door" is necessary but not a sufficient level of family engagement (Wagner et al., 2003, p. 185). Recommended practices in early intervention are designed to engage families *at least* at the application dimension, if not the generalization dimension. It is that highest dimension of engagement where the vision of early intervention is met.

The third point is that these engagement dimensions are not chronological or stepwise. As early intervention has evolved over the last 30 years, most FPPs work within the understanding that "being involved" is the minimal engagement expectation. This condition guides how early intervention is described and how professionals interact with families. Furthermore, as EI professionals work to build family engagement, families do not need to pass through each dimension, moving from present to involved to application and then generalization. Families may begin early intervention at the present level, still uncertain of how to participate. Then, when facilitated by the EI professional, families may move quickly to application and/or generalization. This can occur as early as the first intervention visit. EI professionals identify the current engagement level of each family and intentionally use specific strategies that encourage families to engage at increasingly more active levels (3.1).

WAYS TO PROMOTE FAMILY ENGAGEMENT IN EARLY INTERVENTION

While EI professionals are accustomed to entering into and creating family–professional partnerships, this experience can be quite new for many families. Some families may join this partnership easily and fully right away, while other families will need more time to build a trusting relationship. Many factors affect each family's, and each family member's, readiness to engage, including education level, past experience, income and housing security, community support, and cultural beliefs (Barrera et al., 2012; Beneke & Cheatham, 2016; Hanson & Espinosa, 2016; Hanson & Lynch, 2010; Kalyanpur & Harry, 2012; National Academies, 2016). Early intervention is a very intimate support, working within the family's everyday life and supporting their parenting goals (Fialka, 2001; P. J. McWilliam, 2010). Most families did not expect to need professional supports in fulfilling their parenting role. Some families may feel comfortable with EI practices as the supports they were seeking, while others may feel intimidated or judged (Minke & Scott, 1995). However, EI professionals are responsible for finding ways to engage families in the EI process, most notably by building comfort with the process, focusing on the family's priorities, and working within the family's parenting and partnership style (see Chapter 2). EI professionals can explicitly convey their goals and intention to understand and support rather than judge (Mahoney, Spiker, & Boyce, 1996; R. A. McWilliam et al., 2011).

Building family engagement is a developmental process that evolves over time as families feel more comfortable contributing to the FPP (James & Chard, 2010). While the degree or dimension of family engagement may be evolutionary, EI professionals are responsible for creating a context that supports sustained family engagement from the beginning. Recommendations from research and practical literature (Heffron, Ivins, & Weston, 2005; Keilty, 2008, 2016) say that family engagement is facilitated when EI professionals do the following:

- Express an attitude of caring
- Set shared expectations
- Assure interventions are relevant to family priorities
- Implement interventions that expect family engagement

Though promoting the engagement process is multidimensional, engagement is also fundamental and heartfelt.

Express an Attitude of Caring (3.2)

Families learn about early intervention just as they encounter the unexpected news that their child faces developmental challenges. At the same time, families are learning about a system, a constellation of disciplines, and how to navigate multiple relationships with EI and other professionals. Sometimes, EI professionals can become so focused on the immediacy of promoting child development that the emotional aspect of parenting a child with developmental delays or disabilities is forgotten (Brotherson et al., 2010; Lee, 2015). Fostering engagement requires EI professionals to balance and blend each family's need for information and strategies with emotional support and care (R. A. McWilliam & Scott, 2001).

Caring reflects the professional's connection to the family, just like the family connects with early intervention through engagement. Nel Noddings (2013) wrote about "ethical caring," which built upon a foundation of natural caring, a belief that feeling supersedes reason alone as a basis of ethical action. In early intervention, ethical caring translates into valuing relationships with families guided by the "one caring"—the EI professional—and taking in the perspectives of those "cared-for"—the family. Noddings wrote, "When the other's reality becomes a real possibility to me, I care" (2013, p. 14). This is also known as *empathy*. EI professionals demonstrate care when they do the following (Noddings, 2013):

- Listen to what they hear *and* feel, and take note of what is left unsaid
- Begin with the families' perspectives
- Stay alert to their own feelings and the families' feelings
- Integrate what they know with what they feel as learning happens within relationships

A caring stance is reflected in the relational practices of family–systems interventions that prioritize the beliefs that all people have strengths, can learn, and can become more competent (Dunst & Trivette, 1996; Dunst et al., 2007). Basically, EI professionals show they care about the family by seeing the world from the family members' perspectives. For example, an EI professional might visit the playground and see various developmental opportunities for a child. The child's family might visit a playground and see many typically developing children swinging, digging in the sandbox, and chasing each other freely—without the need for an EI professional alongside the family.

The sensitive EI professional tunes into the family members' experiences, and then reframes the situation to provide useful information, strategies, and supports (Fialka, 2001). Sensing the family's discomfort, the EI professional can reflect, *How do I see this situation differently from the family?* The EI professional takes in the family's perspective by asking questions like, "What would you like to be able to do here? What would you like your child to be able to do here?" Or, if the relationship permits, the EI professional might ask, "How comfortable are you being here? How comfortable are you with me being here with you?" The responses to these questions shape the focus of intervention. EI professionals incorporate care into their work by collaborating as thinking and feeling individuals (3.2.1).

When a family first enters early intervention, they may not have yet processed their feelings, identified questions, or formed opinions to share with EI professionals (Fialka, 2001; James & Chard, 2010). Engagement might be challenging. So what can EI professionals do? Professionals can apply lessons learned from dyadic therapeutic (Fraiberg, 1987) and reflective practices (Gilkerson & Shahmoon-Shanok, 2000; Heffron et al., 2005) that integrate the disciplines of infant mental health, early intervention, and home visiting by using the practices identified below (Geller, 2015; Heffron et al., 2005; Fraiberg, 1987):

- Create an atmosphere of safety for the family by being conscious of any judgmental attitudes the professional might convey, such as identifying the family as defensive or in denial.
- Practice "affective attunement" (Geller & Foley, 2009) by recognizing boundaries, being warm and friendly but thoughtful about when to initiate discussions about feelings, and accepting the family's emotions and ambiguous behaviors as part of the relationship-building process (Brotherson et al., 2010).
- Observe and comment on child and family strengths, including how those strengths connect.

Engagement through care requires listening between the words (Gilkerson & Shamoon-Shanok, 2000). This can be uncomfortable for some professionals as they may not feel prepared to engage in or address families' emotional needs (Brotherson et al., 2010; Heffron et al., 2005). EI professionals recognize care as a professionally valuable attitude, and seek out supports, if needed, to feel confident and competent in conveying a caring attitude (3.2.2).

Set Shared Expectations (3.3)

From the very first visit, EI professionals promote engagement by sharing with families both the EI approach *and* the rationale for that approach. Families might have different expectations of how early intervention works, based on their experiences with other professionals or how early intervention was previously explained (Keilty, 2008, 2016). Together, the FPP explores the importance of routine activities and family-identified outcomes, and collaboratively creates developmental strategies that, through coaching and consultation approaches, result in the family effectively using those strategies (i.e., fidelity) between intervention visits (R. A. McWilliam, 2010a, 2016). Together, the FPP explores the importance of identifying and achieving family and parenting outcomes so the family has the time and focus to help their child learn. EI professionals explore with families how early intervention works, ensure that families understand and appreciate these expectations, and then revisit these concepts as needed should family engagement wane (3.3.1).

However, shared expectations do not result solely from the family's understanding how early intervention works. A reciprocal understanding is needed by the EI professional—appreciating how early intervention fits into the family's conceptions of parenting, child development, and disability. For example, EI professionals struggle when families believe and accept that they only have so much control over child outcomes or the impact of disability (i.e., external locus of control; Al Khateeb et al., 2015; Brotherson et al., 2010; Cheatham & Santos, 2009). This perspective seems counter to the assumptions underlying early intervention and, subsequently, the role of the EI professional, such as "the earlier the better" and "interventions can shift developmental trajectories" (Brotherson et al., 2010; Kalyanpur & Harry, 2012). If EI professionals try to work within these prevailing assumptions, family engagement might falter since the family does not share the same assumptions. Instead, EI professionals can reframe early intervention to fit the family's belief systems, thereby increasing engagement. For example, EI professionals might discuss with families how they believe young children learn and minimize discussions around specific delays or "intervening." In other words, EI professionals situate early intervention within the families' perceptions of parenting, child development, and disability rather than trying to convince families to change their beliefs to fit early intervention (3.3.2).

Assure Family Relevance (3.4)

When early intervention is designed specifically for what the family is interested in, the family is more likely to engage. Research found that family engagement is highest during intervention visits when the intervention focuses specifically on child development or family functioning (Peterson et al., 2007). In other words, family engagement is promoted when EI professionals explicitly attend to what families came to early intervention for—the family's priorities and outcomes, during the particular times the family is looking for EI support (i.e., family-identified routine activities)—and assure progress toward meeting those priorities and outcomes is seen by both FPP members (3.4.1).

To identify these outcomes, EI professionals pair professional knowledge and a commitment to care when asking the family about their child and family and learning about the family's everyday life. Sometimes families will clearly state their expected outcomes. Other times, the EI professional will wonder out loud (e.g., "it sounds like you might like to . . . ") to elicit outcomes from the family's comments. This "wondering together" promotes engagement and begins to generate synchrony between the FPP gears. This process does not occur just once, but is reassessed at each intervention visit, recognizing the fluid nature of family life. At the beginning of each visit, EI professionals assure that supports are relevant and timely by asking families to identify the focus (i.e., priorities) for that particular visit (3.4.2).

Family Engagement Dimensions and Practices   45

Sometimes, families and EI professionals may appear to be working from seemingly disparate outcomes. For example, perhaps a family wants their child to learn how to do puzzles, a play task common in some families. However, the EI professional perceives potentially complex reasons underlying the child's disinterest in puzzles. The EI professional builds engagement with the family by sharing those reasons and identifying the steps that both address the child's disinterest in puzzles and lead to the completion of puzzles. Of course, the family still needs to understand and value the connection and not feel pressured to simply accept the professional's rationale. Therefore, EI professionals observe child behaviors and wonder with families to commingle professional-identified developmental expectations with family expectations to create meaningful interventions in which families want to engage (3.4.3) (Heffron et al., 2005).

Intervention relevance also includes compatibility between the strategies used to meet those outcomes and the individual family culture. For example, an EI professional might believe that a structured behavioral approach would be a good fit to redirect a child's behavior, but the family feels uncomfortable with the approach, considering it too controlling. As discussed in Chapter 1, EI professionals discuss with the family the active ingredients of potential interventions and together identify ways to modify or substitute interventions to better fit the family's culture, without reducing its effectiveness (3.4.4).

Expect Family Engagement (3.5)

Behaviors consistent with nationally endorsed EI practices promote family engagement. Previous research found that family engagement in home visits increased when the professional coached while the family interacted with the child and when the professional asked questions as opposed to making direct statements (Peterson et al., 2007). Therefore, family engagement, defined by the family's interest, initiation, elaboration, questioning, and active participation, occurred specifically when EI professionals interacted with the family in ways that elicited these engagement expectations.

These participatory practices create a shared focus, encourage families to make intervention decisions, and subsequently promote family confidence and competence (Dunst & Espe-Scherwindt, 2016). The relationship of these practices to family engagement makes sense as families engage when they are actively a part of intervention. If one is not participating, one might feel not needed or useful, and therefore disengage. Dunst and Trivette (1996) described participatory experiences as "bring[ing] collective wisdom and knowledge to bear on solutions to problems and attainment of desired outcomes" (p. 334). This sharing of ideas, information, and strategies is engagement. When this process works, a deeper collaboration develops which is intrinsically rewarding for both partnership members. EI professionals can do certain things to create this engagement:

- Explicitly describe the rationale behind specific approaches recommended
- Acknowledge and value the different perspectives families and EI professionals bring to the FPP
- Express confidence that, through these different perspectives, common agreement can be reached

Dunst and Espe-Sherwindt (2016) specifically identified family choice and professional flexibility as participatory practices that promote family engagement. As identified above, when interventions are aligned to family expectations, desires, and interests, the family will be more apt to engage. Creating this alignment occurs when families have choices in the areas of intervention (e.g., priorities and outcomes), how intervention occurs (e.g., strategies, professionals involved, and intensity), and where intervention occurs (e.g., routine activities). To intervene according to family choice, EI professionals are flexible to meet the diversity of choices families make. Therefore, EI professionals value family choice around EI outcomes, approaches, and strategies, and provide interventions according to the choices each family makes (3.5.1).

EI professionals may worry about engagement waning between EI visits. At these times, technology can be used. For example, through texting, EI professionals ask questions and offer support, encouragement, and information to sustain engagement. Technology can also be used to connect with family members who attend intervention visits less frequently. For example, when intervention visits occur primarily during the weekday and a parent or family member is not available during that time, EI professionals can connect with family member(s) via technology. However, EI professionals must keep in mind that, while one family member might find communication by text safe, another might find it impersonal. As with all approaches, EI professionals ask families how they wish to communicate between visits and use those modes to nurture engagement (3.5.2).

Since the child and family change over time, there is no one formula for sustaining engagement once it is formed. But, when the EI professional and family openly acknowledge their interdependence, a relationship is in place to sustain engagement when obstacles arise or when roles evolve. As James and Chard (2010) noted, "partnerships are developmental and grow over time, representing a shift in the roles and responsibilities of each of the players" (p. 281). The elements of engagement described above are foundational to not only initially shaping but also maintaining engagement in the FPP throughout the course of early intervention: emotional connections and care, shared expectations, family relevance of outcomes and approaches, and engagement behaviors.

PAIRED REFLECTIONS AND LESSONS LEARNED: DEVELOPMENT OF ENGAGEMENT

The paired reflections of Kat, a physical therapist, and Rashonda, a mother whose family is supported by early intervention, provide practical evidence of many of the concepts described in this chapter. Kat's reflections fundamentally identify what she expects from herself, and also the profound rewards she garners from what she is able to provide for family engagement. She makes it seem simple. Rashonda's experience conveys the uniqueness intrinsic to the very personal and more emotional experience from the family perspective. It is the professional's job; it is the family's heart.

Kat shared her reflections in written form. Rashonda shared her reflections with Bonnie Keilty on the phone. These reflections were woven together, alternating family and professional reflections, to reveal the spiral nature of engagement, the power of family–professional partnership, and the impact of collaboration on child and family outcomes. Readers can note the successful points of contact—or lessons learned—to build and sustain family engagement.

Lesson Learned: Listen with Heart and Mind (3.6)

Professional Reflection: Listen First. Families . . . come in confused at times as to why they were referred and unsure if their problems will be heard. So when Aprillyon, his mother, and his aunt crammed into the room with the developmental specialist, service coordinator, and me, the family was unsure if they could trust us since they felt that no one was listening to their concerns thus far. The family gave me consent to hold their little baby so I could play and evaluate the need for therapy. The family questioned if they were overreacting to some concerns, but brought them up anyway. All I did was listen to their concerns while engaging with the baby.

Family Reflection: I Needed Someone to Listen with Heart and Mind. [I was told that my family wouldn't be eligible for early intervention.] But I was just very adamant . . . they're wrong with Aprillyon. And so this one lady out of the bunch of women that were there, she just took the baby. . . . She just took off his clothes and she just started examining him and looking him up from top to bottom. And I was just sitting there observing, and . . . right then and there, I knew her heart was pure and she loved what she did. . . . You know, on the outside . . . when you first looked at him you saw, like, he's a normal child. But in my head, something in my heart just kept telling me to ask for help for this baby.

Family Reflection: Someone Listened! There were these little nodules on his body. . . . I had never seen it in a newborn. The hospitals kept telling me that everything was okay with the baby. I took him to three different hospitals before we went to early intervention and finally when we get there, this lady actually listened to what I'm trying to tell her.

Kat's responses to Rashonda embodied an *attitude of professional caring*, which guided her professional actions. Kat identified Rashonda's uncertainty and her need to develop trust with these particular EI professionals. That awareness guided Kat's *relational action* of listening to Rashonda's concerns with an open mind.

Lesson Learned: Prioritize the Family's Questions (3.7)

Professional Reflection: Address Concerns. I then addressed their concerns to the best of my abilities, and told them that they knew the baby best, and asked if there was anything I could do to facilitate getting their message and concerns addressed to obtain the services they needed. [Kat then provided Rashonda with written notes.] Not knowing where to begin, I made some suggestions to bring back to their pediatricians, made my recommendations for physical therapy and other services to evaluate.

Family Reflection: She Looked at the Person Not the Paperwork. [The other professionals were] . . . going off the paperwork. And because they were going off the paperwork instead of going off of the child and what I was telling them, how I felt as a parent, . . . they were just reading the hospital paperwork. . . . They didn't hear me out, and my concern for my child. That's when I felt—like this other woman [Kat]—she just sat down, and she just really tuned everybody else out. Without paperwork, without anything, and she tuned into the baby. And when she did that, she noticed a lot of things. Everything I was saying. [She said,] "Mom has valid concerns. This baby does have nodules all over his body. . . . His right arm has contracted all the way." . . . I had been trying to address [this] to doctors . . . for months. She [addressed it]. . . . Because of that, if he never would have made that first connection [with early intervention], I believe we would never have been this far in our journey. . . . That was an "oh my god" moment. Somebody hears me!

Family Reflection: Communication, Information, and Advocacy. [Without Kat], my son would never have gotten the help he needed. The doctors would not have listened to me. They would never have found out he was diagnosed with this rare disease. . . . My baby probably still wouldn't be alive. That's how serious it was, . . . and that's just how much communication meant right from the start. She paid attention to everything that came out of my mouth.

If you don't understand something, to have someone break it down in terms where you understand it, it's just such a relief as a parent. A lot of terminology the doctors throw at you, you're like "Huh? I don't understand" or "What? What does that mean?" And you go to a person who understands it and they break it down in terms where you understand. It's just a great relief.

It was almost as if she was an advocate. It was like she was advocating for my son just as hard as I was. And when she entered the case [she said,] "I wouldn't do [anything] . . . different than I would do for my own child." I just thought I had never heard a person say that to me.

Family Reflection: Feeling Lost, Feeling Found. Because me coming into this as a parent, when you find out information like this, you're lost. You don't know what to do and who to turn to. And I think she's seen a lot of confusion within me being lost and my heart was already broken. . . . It wasn't even in her job description. She went above and beyond her job to make sure that my son . . . got the help he needed and guided me to some people that can help me. . . . She's the one that coached me and helped build me and encourage me to keep advocating for my son.

When Kat first encountered Rashonda's family, they were still seeking information and professional partners who could help them navigate through a medical system that had been resistant to addressing their needs. Kat wrote down her observations so Rashonda could take the document to various hospitals, reversing the dismissive reception she had previously experienced. Thus began the process of diagnosis and treatment. In this action, Kat partnered with Rashonda to promote empowerment so Rashonda could act upon her priority and gain the immediate medical attention needed.

Rashonda also expressed what it meant to be heard by Kat—a great relief that the doctors began to take her concerns seriously and to obtain the medical information in a way that allowed Rashonda to understand and advocate. By listening, Kat communicated respect. As a translator of complex medical terminology, she communicated information in a way so Rashonda could achieve a deeper understanding, relieving her uncertainty and emboldening her action.

By prioritizing the family's questions, Kat communicated, provided information, and both advocated and supported Rashonda in advocating. Rashonda was always ready to be fully engaged, and was waiting for an EI partner who could reciprocally engage by integrating an attitude of caring and professional knowledge.

Lesson Learned: Trust in the Partnership and All Partnership Members (3.8)

Professional Reflection: A Relationship Built on Trust. Due to listening and taking care when playing with their baby at the initial consult, the family was able to trust me enough to invite me into their home. As a result of building this trust between therapist and family, (a) the family was able to become fully engaged from the beginning and had excellent follow-through with all the exercises; (b) the family slowly became empowered and were able to search and reach out to the right people to assist in caring for Aprillyon's medical needs; and (c) the family transitioned into a powerful advocate for their child so that finally family and therapist were able to reciprocally educate and teach each other about his medical needs and care.

Family Reflection: Trust and Valued Qualities of Communication. [Aprillyon's early intervention team was formed, with Kat as a member.] When[ever] I had questions, no matter what time of the night or morning they would answer the phone. They would pop up at the hospitals. It was just an incredible responsive support. I was blown back. . . . I have never seen a group of ladies put so much heart into their job. . . . Any questions I had, if they didn't know, they would never give me an answer until they found or got that right answer . . . or someone who could help me. They never put me on the back burner and let me sit. . . . They were always very direct.

Family Reflection: The EI Process—A Team Is Behind You. So the first part of the early intervention process was to teach me about my son's illness and educate me on . . . how they were going to try to help—even if I didn't understand it. Then they would help me research it . . . like, "Go Google this." . . . And that's how I got educated on the terminology, "No, this is how you say it." . . . So from the first time I went to UCLA [to] about the second or third time, the doctors can tell I had educated myself. Someone happened to teach me; someone had been helping me to keep this baby alive and it just wasn't the doctors here.

Professional Reflection: A Privileged Position. So, basically it comes down to the families entrusting us, not only with their children, but giving us the privilege to be part of their team, and really part of their family. We are another "dynamic"—they have to figure out how we fit into their already crazy lives. [With this family,] I was fortunate enough that I was respectful to their needs and allowed them to "vent" in a way, because they felt like no one else was listening. This is a gift whenever I get to interact with any family—that they invite me into their lives, and not just their home.

Family Reflection: Part of the Family. [Kat] is more than his physical therapist. . . . She makes sure the whole family engages in Aprillyon's therapy and what is going on, and educate us as a family how to help Aprillyon.

[When Kat thought Aprillyon was nearly ready to learn how to roll and move on the floor,] she taught the brothers on the floor how he was going to move around. And then, from them moving around on the floor and showing Aprillyon the moves, he started rolling around on the floor. . . . But you have to really understand the process. For a baby that can't move, [to] really want to go, they're going to try . . . so Kat taught the baby how to roll.

. . . I have this on video! [Kat told the boys] . . . to keep rolling around [Aprillyon] and all of a sudden, the baby started rolling. And that was the first movement he ever did. And that's when the doctors knew . . . he was going to get up. And that's when we started getting equipment. . . . Until then, we never got anything. Anything—until I showed them the video that my baby was moving.

As their relationship developed, Kat's approach to empowerment was characterized by a partnership with Rashonda where each partnership member brought their strengths to meeting the family's priorities. Kat trusted that Rashonda and her family could address Aprillyon's medical needs once the medical terminology was interpreted for them. As a validating participant, Kat amplified Rashonda's voice with less responsive professionals she encountered elsewhere. Because of this, Rashonda's family developed a trust that allowed them to utilize Kat's professional knowledge to meet their needs.

Kat acknowledged that she felt welcomed into the family. But she also actively engaged the family in early intervention. Using her knowledge of development and her professional discipline, she had a sense of when Aprillyon would be ready to roll. She integrated elements of how he learns, the motivating value of his brothers, and the pure joy of movement. Subsequently, Rashonda used the videotape of his performance to obtain needed equipment. That is the very definition of engagement for both partnership members—motivated, interested, and active participants in achieving the family's goals.

CONCLUSION: FAMILY ENGAGEMENT DIMENSIONS AND PRACTICES

As Kat and Rashonda's fully engaged relationship illustrates, engagement relies upon both partners' readiness to participate. But, just think, *what if* Kat had not listened so carefully? She might have unintentionally reduced Rashonda's engagement, making it more difficult to build a trusting family–professional partnership. Therefore, Kat's commitment to caring and sensitive practices were essential skills to promote engagement. As Rashonda said,

At the end, with the positive thinking of a positive team and a knowledgeable team, your child will go far. There are endless possibilities as long as you guys are on the same communication page. As long as you want it for your child and that person understands what you want for your child, I feel like the partnership will go far.

> **QUESTIONS FOR DAILY REFLECTION**
>
> 1. How did each family take the initiative during my visits? What kind of information was each family seeking?
> 2. Reflecting upon a feeling I experienced in my work with families today, how did I respond in the moment? What would I do the same or different next time?
> 3. How did I identify each family's priorities for the day? How were those priorities similar to or different from what I expected to address today?
> 4. What level of engagement would I use to describe each family in today's visits? What steps led me to that engagement level? For any families who are not engaging at the generalization level, what will I do to support the family in getting to the generalization level?

CHAPTER 4

Family and Professional Power Players

Bonnie Keilty and Hedi Levine

Consider trying to paddle a canoe with a partner who strokes with different force. What happens? The canoe travels in circles. Now consider what happens when the power with which they paddle is equal. Those same two paddlers propel the canoe forward to where they want it to go. In early intervention, family and professional partners contribute equal amounts of *power* to meet their shared goals.

POWER IN PARTNERSHIPS

Power is the ability to influence what others do or think, as well as the achievement of specific aims, such as Individualized Family Service Plan (IFSP) outcomes. Turnbull and colleagues (2015) defined power as "the ability and intention to use authority, influence, or control over others" (p. 175). These words might seem negative or controlling at first. However, power is energy—energy to act. Therefore, power is needed to make change happen. How individuals use that power, and how others perceive that power, can be positive or impeding (Spino et al., 2013). In early intervention, both families and professionals bring positive power to the family–professional partnership. These powers are acknowledged, appreciated, and harnessed.

Power is somewhat different from strengths. Strengths are concrete contributions—the family's knowledge of their child or the professional's toolbox of strategies—used to achieve a goal, namely, EI outcomes. Power is more intangible but no less important. Power is the force that propels an individual or, in this case, a family–professional partnership, to use their strengths to shape the partnership, what each partnership member does, and, subsequently, the outcomes of that partnership. The following sections explore the power that families and professionals bring to achieve their EI goals.

POWER OF THE FAMILY

The power of the family comes from the influence they have as their children's most significant developmental promoters. This influence results from the deep connection to their children, the unmistakable influence of parent–child interactions, and the inseparable nature of the child as a member of the family.

The Power of Connection

At the turn of the century, noted child psychologist Urie Bronfenbrenner spoke about what the "21st-century baby" needs developmentally. He identified the same types of quality interactions as their 20th-century predecessors, adding the now frequently quoted line, "Somebody's got to be crazy about that kid!" (Bronfenbrenner, 2002, p. 46). However, it is his further explanation that so clearly illustrates the power of the connection between the child and the family:

> Any family of course knows that his or her child is not the most intelligent, the most beautiful, the most wonderful in the world. Nevertheless, at some level deep inside, that is what most of us feel—that our own children are more *magical and special* than any other children we know. (Bronfenbrenner, 2002, p. 46, emphasis added)

This quote conveys the importance (i.e., power) to child development that families are so connected, so captivated with their children that families will "go to bat" for them (see "Family Reflections" below). Maximizing child outcomes *depends* on families feeling this way. And yet, families in early intervention are frequently confronted with words that assign negative characteristics to their children. Families come to, and are eligible for, early intervention due to a *concern*. Early intervention is provided to reduce or ameliorate the impact of developmental *delay* or *disability*. These words contradict the perspective that their child is "more magical and special than any other." These words can impede the development of a positive FPP when families feel the professionals do not hold their same opinion. How do EI professionals work to support this positive perception?

Strengths-based interventions (SBI) have long been applied to EI practice (e.g., Dunst & Espe-Sherwindt, 2016; Dunst & Trivette, 2009a; P. J. McWilliam, 2010). In SBI, EI professionals recognize and utilize the child's developmental assets—what the child knows and does, and what the child is interested in and motivated by—to enhance overall competence. EI professionals identify and communicate at least an equal number of developmental strengths as developmental needs (Jung & McWilliam, 2005). Using the term "needs" instead of "weaknesses" shifts from a deficit internal to the child to a support expected from the outside world. These approaches convey to families that their children are, indeed, "magical and special." EI professionals can further preserve the positive perception by using the following:

Frame early intervention as a developmental promotion program (4.1). Instead of early intervention being positioned as a corrective or remedial model (e.g., "to address developmental concerns"), early intervention can be described as a program to "help children learn" or, more specifically, "to help families help their children to learn."

Use words and actions that reflect the developmental promotion frame (4.2). EI professionals can reflect on the particular words used and actions taken during the EI process and weigh the impact of those words and actions on the family's perceptions of their child. For example, instead of focusing on the child's developmental status as delayed, EI professionals can identify the child's current abilities—no matter how different from typical developmental expectations—as the foundation from which to build new abilities.

Use assessment instruments that allow for flexible administration to demonstrate the extent of child abilities while minimizing items inappropriate for the child to attempt (4.3). Many assessment instruments outline procedures that do not fit the developmental profiles of young children in early intervention whose abilities and needs are "scattered" versus adhering to a continuous developmental progression. When these instruments are used, the child may be exposed to, and the family may be witnesses to, the "failure" of items that do not contribute to the developmental picture needed for intervention planning. Instead, professionals can use instruments like criterion-based measures on which they can omit items inappropriate for the child to attempt and uncover advanced abilities in other areas.

Use open-ended assessment instruments and less-structured procedures to gather assessment data from families (4.4). When EI professionals ask families to complete rating scales, there is a risk that any low scores the family assigns to items can diminish their magical and special perception. Alternatively, to preserve this positive perception, families might choose not to use the lower range of scores, even though the family knows certain items should be scored in that range. In this instance, reliability and validity is diminished and professionals might perceive the family to be "in denial" (see Chapter 6).

Note that neither strengths-based interventions nor these additional recommendations suggest that professionals withhold information or alter the accuracy of their understanding of the child's strengths and needs. It's about how that information is presented in order to maintain the power of the family, create an FPP built on optimism, and preserve the family being "crazy about that kid!"

The Power of Parent-Child Interactions

Quality interactions between adult family members—most particularly, parents—and their children positively impact cognitive, social, communicative, and literacy outcomes (e.g., Dodici, Draper, & Peterson, 2003; Innocenti et al., 2013; Kong & Carta, 2013). Furthermore, the power of quality parent–child interaction lies in its significant influence on EI effectiveness (Mahoney et al., 1998; Institute of Medicine, 2000; Raikes et al., 2014). Research analyzing intervention data found the effects of the intervention depended on the use of positive parental interaction strategies (Mahoney et al., 1998). In an Early Head Start evaluation, quality interactions—including supportiveness, responsiveness, and language and cognitive stimulation—mediated program impact on child outcomes at 36 months (Raikes et al., 2014). Therefore, interventions focused solely on child outcomes are insufficient. Instead, to maximize intervention effectiveness, <u>EI professionals blend strategies that both enhance quality parent–child interaction and child developmental outcomes within the multiple opportunities afforded in everyday family life (4.5)</u> (Innocenti et al., 2013; Kong & Carta, 2013; Institute of Medicine, 2000; Raab et al., 2013; Trivette et al., 2013).

Specific strategies that comprise positive interactions are those responsive caregiving approaches of warmth or sensitivity, consistent and contingent responsiveness, and approaches to engage the child in learning (Bronfenbrenner, 1999, 2002; Dodici et al., 2003; Dunst & Trivette, 2009c; Innocenti et al., 2013; Keilty & Galvin, 2006; Kim & Mahoney, 2004; Kong & Carta, 2013; National Academies, 2016). When children are typically developing, the child usually provides clear communicative cues to which the adult family member can respond. For families of children with disabilities, responsive caregiving can be more difficult as the child's interactive cues can be different from or more subtle than expected, making them harder to identify, understand, and respond to (Innocenti et al., 2013; Keilty & Freund, 2005; Khetani et al., 2013; Smyth et al., 2014). Recognizing the power of parent–child interaction, <u>EI professionals analyze the goodness of fit of the family's responsive caregiving approaches to the child's interaction style and, if needed, partner with the family to enhance those approaches to foster powerful relationships (4.6)</u>.

The Power of the Child as a Member of a Family

The child cannot be separated from the context in which the child lives, learns, and grows—his or her family. The power of the family is seen in the direct and indirect influences of family functioning on parent–child interaction and child development (Bailey, Raspa, & Fox, 2012; Dunst et al., 2007; Trivette et al., 2010). To harness this power, EI professionals can use the following practices:

Identify and facilitate the achievement of family outcomes as a means to family quality of life (4.7). Family quality of life—including feeling good about themselves, having positive relationships and informal support systems, and feeling secure emotionally and financially—is important in and of itself as well as for its influence on child development (Bailey et al., 2012; Dunst et al., 2007; Epley, Summers, & Turnbull, 2011; Kresak, Gallagher, & Kelley, 2014; Trivette et al., 2010; Turnbull et al., 2015; Wainer, Hepburn, & Griffith, 2016). Outcomes that address family needs are expected to contribute to family quality of life (Bailey et al., 2012; Epley et al, 2011). These outcomes include those desired for the entire family and those related to parenting their child, in addition to those specifically related to the child's learning and development.

Recognize and respond to the needs of families of children with developmental delays or disabilities (4.8) (Bailey et al., 2012). This may seem counter to the earlier recommendation of preserving the family's positive perceptions of their child. However, consider some of the needs a family with a typically developing child might have: the need to find child care or ways to afford quality child care; the need to find others with similar age children for playdates. These needs do not negate the positive qualities of their child. At the same time, ignoring the real challenges families face when raising a child with developmental delays or disabilities can be discouraging, especially from professionals who are in the family's life because of these needs (Lee, 2015). EI professionals hold positive perceptions of the child and family while simultaneously acknowledging and addressing disability-related needs.

Promote family self-efficacy versus dependence (4.9). Self-efficacy is a sense of belief in oneself to be able to meet family, parenting, and child outcomes (Karst & Van Hecke, 2012; National Academies, 2016). Parenting self-efficacy, fostered by strengths-based interventions, has been found to have direct effects on parent–child interaction and child development outcomes (Dunst et al., 2007; National Academies, 2016; Trivette et al., 2010). EI professionals work in ways that foster self-efficacy by articulating and acting from a belief in the capacity of families to understand their own and their child's needs; to identify the approaches that already work for them; and to make informed decisions about how to address current and future priorities (Bryan, 2014).

Earlier in this chapter, power and strengths were differentiated. Families bring to the FPP the strengths of knowing and understanding their child and organizing learning opportunities for their child through the materials, strategies, and routine activities of their everyday life (Guralnick, 2011; Keilty, 2016). The power described above illustrates the intensity of families' influence on their children and child development which, in turn, conveys the intensity of power each family holds in the FPP to meet its early intervention goals.

POWER OF THE PROFESSIONAL

The power of the EI professional is probably easier to identify than the power of the family. Professionals, by definition, have the power to act according to their profession. Ship captains chart the course, police officers direct traffic, and judges make rulings. In early intervention, professionals' power comes from their expertise and role, and their relationship to institutions of authority. This power is positively used when it is harnessed to support the family to use their power.

The Power of the Expert

The holding of deep knowledge and skills is powerful. EI professionals come to the family–professional partnership with specialized education and training, culminating in their expertise to implement early intervention. This expertise endows upon professionals the power to form impressions about developmental strengths and needs and, subsequently, devise and evaluate strategies to promote development. EI professionals also come to the FPP with knowledge of the influence of culture, family systems in general, and ways to understand and support each family in meeting their family, parenting, and child outcomes. EI professionals utilize expert power in a manner that is individualized according to child strengths and needs, family priorities, and the characteristics of everyday family life (4.10).

The Power of the Institution

EI professionals arrive at a family's door as representatives of influential institutions. They are agents of federal and state governments and local EI programs whose policies guide EI implementation. The EI system also has its own beliefs, values, language (e.g., IFSP, natural environments), and ways of work, including home visiting, teaming, and coaching (Kalyanpur & Harry, 2012). EI professionals are enculturated into this system from their professional education; they share a perspective that becomes "assumed" or understood as a "way to look at things." To apply this power positively, EI professionals can use the following practices:

Recognize that institutions hold power and EI professionals represent those institutions (4.11). EI professionals may not feel like they have power. They may feel that the power of the institution affects them as much as the families. However, there is power in being associated with the system that authorizes the desired supports, knowing how the system works, and understanding the EI "culture" (Hanson & Espinosa, 2016). EI professionals recognize institutional power so they can mitigate its potential to create a power disparity between family and professional partnership members.

Employ professional power to navigate the early intervention system (4.12).
EI professionals translate the early intervention "culture" for families in the following ways:

- Transforming family rights into meaningful privileges
- Supporting families in identifying questions for other professionals in and out of early intervention
- Applying developmental frameworks to specific family questions about their individual child rather than providing generalized developmental information that the family then has to decipher
- Partnering with the family to effectively advocate for the child and family within the early intervention and other systems
- Coaching the family in the forms and processes of EI, special education, and medical and social service systems in ways that build family capacity to navigate these systems after early intervention

The Power of the Role

The responsibility of creating an effective FPP lies with the EI professional (Harbin, McWilliam, & Gallagher, 2000). The EI professional builds and conveys a true FPP by reflecting and responding to families (Barerra et al., 2012). By doing so, power is shared and utilized. In other words, the power inherent to the EI professional's role is to facilitate family *empowerment*. An empowerment ideology welcomes all families, assumes people are already competent, directs power to generate opportunities for the family to experience their competence, and conveys a sincere appreciation of the family's value (Beneke & Cheatham, 2016; Dunst, Trivette, Davis, & Cornwell, 1988; Krauss, 2000). To apply role power positively, EI professionals use the following practices:

Explicitly discuss and act on the family's strengths and power (4.13). Bringing attention to the family's strengths and power illuminates for the family their contributions to the FPP. This can result in both promoting family self-efficacy and equalizing power (P. J. McWilliam, 2010).

Provide unbiased information for the family so they can make informed decisions (4.14). EI professionals provide families with information, including the reasons behind any recommended actions to be taken. If the information makes sense to the family, they will integrate and continue to use the information provided (Spino et al., 2013). In other words, the expert power is shared within the role power (of empowerment), taking care not to overly influence the family as they make their decisions (Sass-Lehrer, Porter, & Wu, 2016; Turnbull et al., 2015). Instead, EI professionals support the family by providing them with unbiased information, understanding the family's reasons for the specific actions they choose to take, and working from the family's decision.

Recognize and remedy when role and expertise power conflict (4.15).
Embracing a professional orientation toward empowerment directs the professional's use of power to "focus on strategies by which families use assistance to identify and achieve self-defined goals" (Krauss, 2000, p. 296). Sometimes, EI professionals may feel families are not utilizing the professional's expert power in the decisions that they make. For example, EI professionals may see opportunities for intervention in the daily lives of families—how routines are structured, language is used, environments arranged, or a task is presented. Once the professional shares the opportunities, the family may decide to act on some or none of the information shared. At these times, professionals are careful not to convey a power-over perspective, such as making decisions or overly influencing the family in their decisions (Sass-Lehrer et al., 2016; Turnbull et al., 2015). Instead, professionals recognize the power of self-efficacy and support families as they make decisions by focusing on the aspects of change the family is motivated to make (Deci & Ryan, 2000; Ryan, Deci, Fowler, Seligman, & Csikszentmihalyi, 2000; Williams, Rodin, Ryan, Grolnick, & Deci, 1998).

Alternatively, there may be times when the expert power the family is seeking is not the power the EI professional feels most comfortable using. For example, a family might be discussing with professionals some aspect of family life that suggests a family outcome or emotional need is unmet. Depending on their background, some EI professionals may feel uncomfortable or unprepared to support families in these areas (Brotherson et al., 2010). They may try to keep the focus on the child, where their expert power lies. However, considering their role power, EI professionals must focus the intervention on the family's current priorities, including family and parenting outcomes.

Professionals use their power, combined with all the other FPP concepts, to help the family achieve their goals in ways that are comfortable for them (Engster, 2005; Ylitapio-Mantylä, 2013).

SHARING POWER

In looking at the power brought by families and professionals, it may seem like the professional is more powerful. The power of the professional's expertise, relationship to EI institutions, and role is strong and potentially intimidating (Sass-Lehrer et al., 2016; Turnbull et al., 2015). Families may naturally give the power to the professional because they are seeking this expertise and support. The perceptions of families, as well as professionals, that professional team members have more power than family members can contribute to an unequal power differential (P. J. McWilliam, 2010; Sass-Lehrer et al., 2016; Spino et al., 2013; Trivette & Dunst, 1987; Turnbull et al., 2015).

This potential power disparity has resulted in EI policies and procedures that attempt to level the power by mandating family participation and consent in EI decisions (Kalyanpur & Harry, 2012). However, the power to truly and fully effect change—to maximize the EI goal of enhancing child development—lies within the power of the family. The professional's power is "instrumental" in that it is really only good if it supports and enhances the family's power. When EI professionals recognize this, the power differential shifts from power-over to power-shared (Bryan, 2014; P. J. McWilliam, 2010; Sass-Lehrer et al., 2016; Turnbull et al., 2015). While families may give their power to the professional, there are ways by which professionals can give the power back to families:

Articulate and act in accordance with the family's power (4.16). EI professionals respect the power families bring, and share this appreciation with each family. Sharing power relies on "co-creation," openness, collaboration, and trust (Sokoly & Dokecki, 1992, p. 29). This expression of shared power is conveyed authentically as families "are especially able to 'see through' helpgivers who act as if they care but don't, and help givers that give the impression that [families] . . . have meaningful choices and decisions when they do not" (Dunst & Trivette, 1996, Conclusion, para. 2).

Use the power of the professional (4.17). EI professionals provide their expertise openly and honestly and situate information and potential decision options within the EI system, while also using their role power to facilitate the family's decision-making process.

Recognize and respond to signs that the family does not feel powerful in the family-professional partnership (4.18). EI professionals are especially attuned to times families cede their power to the professional, most particularly when cultural differences may make partnering more difficult (Barrera et al., 2012). At those times, EI professionals intervene to shift the power to equilibrium, including openly collaborating with the family to identify ways to achieve that balance.

The following professional and family reflections illustrate the balance of power created in this FPP.

PROFESSIONAL REFLECTIONS: VALUING THE POWER OF ALL PARTNERS

Cara, a developmental therapist, shares her reflections of partnering with Judith's family by recognizing and using the power of all the partners.

I had the privilege to share in one family's journey with their precious son, Makai. I met Makai and his family when he was about two months old. He had multiple medical conditions, including vision concerns. With my background as an Orientation and Mobility Specialist, we had many conversations to find ways to encourage Makai to increase his visual awareness. We also addressed feeding concerns, medical needs, and many other concerns the family had for Makai. As the months progressed, Makai's medical needs increased where he needed full-time nursing care in his home. I interacted with the family and other professionals during our visits. I soon realized that we all had important roles in assisting Makai and his family. I believe the family has the most valuable role with their child. Makai's family was also learning how to balance the new relationships with all of the professionals working with Makai.

Over the months and years, I saw that Judith was a very active participant in Makai's intervention strategies (both medical and developmental). Judith asked many questions during our EI visits and offered input on what she thought would benefit Makai. Many times I mentioned something that might be beneficial for Makai, like hanging a picture above his hospital bed in his room, only to find a colorful poster on the ceiling the next week. I observed Judith's same interest in Makai's medical care. She learned the names of all of his medicines and the many medical terms.

I remember visiting Makai and Judith in the hospital during one of Makai's many hospital stays. At this particular visit, the nurse/caseworker wanted to speak with Judith. I asked if I should leave but Judith asked me to stay. The nurse/caseworker began talking to Judith about the severity of Makai's medical condition and the need for a DNR [Do Not Resuscitate]. This was the first time I truly realized the severity of Makai's condition. I was present at a critical time when Judith needed to make an extremely difficult decision. I did not offer my opinion but let her know that I was available to discuss her thoughts.

I had many opportunities to build partnerships with Judith and the daily [in-home] nurses. I was cautious to ensure that Judith was informed of ideas and strategies when I worked with the nurse. I continued to ask Judith questions about her concerns and priorities along with asking the nurses many questions. Sometimes I had part of the visit with Judith and part of the visit with the nurse. Even when I met with the nurse for the entire visit, I talked to Judith on the phone or left a note about the visit.

Judith asked me and the other professionals many questions about her concerns for Makai. She was extremely helpful as she answered the many questions [we professionals] asked about Makai. Judith and her concerns and priorities determined the agenda for our visits. I believe that having the family determine the agenda for each visit is a great way to keep the partnership in balance. By allowing Judith to determine what we addressed at each visit, it ensured that I was not assuming too much power in our relationship. I was also careful not to make assumptions [but to] ask her thoughts on the many issues that we addressed.

When Makai entered into hospice care, we continued to discuss concerns and priorities. There were many difficult times with Makai's medical condition. Judith researched medicines and medical procedures that Makai required. I educated myself on many medicines and procedures, also. I continued to ask Judith questions about Makai's different medical needs to assist her and Makai better. Together we decided what to address each week. Often Makai's medical concerns dictated what we addressed each week. The partnership with the family and caregivers was crucial in finding ways to help Makai.

One of my goals as an early interventionist is to empower families. An important aspect of empowerment is making sure that each person brings power to the relationship. As an early interventionist, I have the opportunity to develop partnerships with each family that I serve. I believe that the family and I both have valuable information to share that can benefit the child. I like to ask the family many open-ended questions during our visits. I learn so much more about the child by asking the family what they have tried and what works and does not work for them. By asking questions, I learn concerns, progress, success, and failures, and so much more. Together, the family and I can determine ways to assist the child when we have open communication.

Makai was a precious little boy; Judith was an amazing mother; and the nurses were so caring and compassionate. I will always treasure the partnership with Makai's mother and his nurses/caregivers. I believe communication and respect were the foundation for the balanced relationship that Judith and I developed. We established our roles at the beginning of the relationship and maintained communication as the needs of the family changed. I respected Judith's priorities for her child. This was a professional relationship, yet it was personal and unique to Judith's family. When other professionals were added to the team, I realized that Judith and the family still maintained the most important role in Makai's life. I also recognized Judith's many strengths and worked to capitalize on those strengths during visits. When we look for wonderful qualities in others, it is not difficult to find them. I look forward to many more partnerships with amazing families.

FAMILY REFLECTIONS: SHARING POWER FOR EMPOWERMENT

Judith, Makai's mother, reflected on sharing power in the early intervention process. These reflections come from the notes taken during a phone conversation between Bonnie Keilty and Judith.

The Power of the Family

One thing that I think is the most important part of [the concept of] power player is that you have to have a receptive family.... [The EI professionals are] not doing it because they're getting a paycheck. [They are] not going through the motions. I think a key part—[you] have to have families who are knowledgeable and a partner. I promise [family members]—you will know your child and you're your child's best advocate.

Judith shared a specific instance when she felt empowered to make, and was subsequently satisfied with the result of, her family's decision when Makai was having seizures. She told the doctors:

"Everybody stop. We are leaving. Stabilize, we need to leave." It was the best decision. I was right. When they said lumbar puncture, I had a feeling it was just not that bad [to warrant a lumbar puncture].... Because I had so many people in my corner telling me, "You're doing great," I felt I could say no.

... There was a time I was educating the doctors about what they should do. They're scratching their heads. [I said], "I'm the liaison for all of you. I promise you, I know what I'm talking about." I had doctors come back to me and say, "You know, you were right."

Using the Power of the Professional

Even though [Cara] wasn't experienced with children like Makai, she knew enough about child development.... It made me feel like, okay well, even though, she's educated in knowing how kids are supposed to respond. She's made a career of working with developmentally delayed children. It made me feel better. We were still feeling [our way] through the dark. It was a journey we got to take together. It made me feel normal.... It made me feel like we're both learning and we're learning at the same pace. It made me feel like equals.... I think that's what made us bond so well—she respected me as here's this family who's going to bat for this kid and working and working. Never giving up.

Sharing Power in Early Intervention Decisions

Identify priorities: What was our definition of quality as far as his development was concerned? That was always the topic of conversation. [The answer was] whatever made his life better, easier, and pleasant. We had to define what our idea of quality was. When he was a tiny baby [the definition was] being alive at any cost. Your idea of quality of life changes when there is a better knowledge of ... development. That's just part of the learning process.

Set goals: One thing that was so essential in my relationship was setting goals and I didn't really know where to begin. I understood his diagnosis and prognosis . . . [but] goals were very difficult to set. [We] started off very basic and very small. . . . Even though I had other children, I was not completely aware of what was age typical. . . . [Cara] was able to inform me . . . [by telling me] "He should be hitting these certain milestones." I was thinking, with his diagnosis, . . . being able to smile [would be a good place to start]. . . . Because of the things I could see him do—he was able to roll over even earlier than typical children—I felt like at that point, seeing what he was able to do, and keeping in mind his neurological diagnosis, we were able to go and pick and choose what developmental milestones were appropriate for him. [Cara] kind of laid it out for me and I thought [smiling] was achievable.

Try out intervention strategies: The one thing I really wanted to get from [Makai]—can I get him to smile. [Cara] had suggested putting on bright red lipstick because it might be a vision issue. Dad put a big sticker on his nose. We worked on it. And within like a month, he was able to do it. . . . We knew at that point, obviously he could see. . . . He was responding to us visually. . . . He sees well enough to see things. [So, we then got him] stimulating toys. We got him mobiles. [Cara] brought brightly colored toys and textured wrapping paper. It was really great to see him respond to any kind of stimulation.

[As we used the strategies to prompt Makai to smile,] Cara encouraged us. . . . [She] made us more cued in to little things—the way he puckered his lips, moved his arms. We knew that he was happy. You wouldn't be able to tell, but we knew through his body language [whether] he was really distressed or happy. That gave us more motivation to keep going with the smile. It's nice to bounce ideas off of somebody.

Power Player Results

[Cara] became part of our family. She experienced the ups and downs of our life. And everything we worked with him on. It was always a success. No matter what the outcome was . . . we were working as a team for him. It's the ideal situation when you have the perfect support group. We were very blessed to have as many caring and intelligent and compassionate people.

[It was] . . . very empowering to feel like the decisions we made were ours. . . . We knew we couldn't do this on our own. We had Cara and a nurse for newborns. . . . As the process grew and he grew, we were introduced to new resources—[we] all did our part. My husband and I . . . felt, "we're doing everything the way we should be. Let's listen to our gut." Like I said, no regrets.

LESSONS LEARNED: POWER PLAYERS

The above reflections demonstrate both family and professional power. Cara described the power of Judith's family in her use of the word "privilege," identification of their "important role," and establishment of a family–professional partnership that is "personal and unique." Judith identified her family's power as an advocate (e.g., "going to bat"), holding a strengths-based perception of Makai, such as noticing that he rolled over earlier than typically expected and used his vision to begin to smile, and recognizing the family's ability to read and respond to his interaction style when distressed or happy. Judith discussed how the FPP collaborated to define quality of life at different points in time and, for their family, the importance of addressing Makai's medical needs.

Both partnership members identified Cara's expert power in child development, special instruction, and orientation and mobility. Her institutional power was available as needed when visiting the hospital. Cara's role power was apparent in Judith's description of how they worked together. Cara was available to "encourage" and "bounce ideas off." These concepts are further described below in the following lessons learned, practices showing how EI professionals share power.

Take the lead in ensuring the family takes the lead (4.19). It's easier for professionals to share power when families use the power of the family. Some families feel comfortable taking initiative right away. Other families are guided by how the professional distributes power. At these latter times, professionals might unintentionally fall into a power-over stance (Turnbull et al., 2015). Cara identified specific strategies she uses with all families to support families in taking the lead—the FPP establishes clear roles, the family sets the agenda for each visit, and the professional uses open-ended questions to convey "I am learning from the family."

Encourage all partners to weigh in on decisions to achieve a "balanced relationship" (4.20) (Kalyanpur & Harry, 2012). Cara used the term "balanced relationship" in her description of the power partnership concept. This idea of balance requires a continual weighing of power to ensure it is indeed equally balanced. In deciding on the outcome of smiling, Cara *weighed in* with potential developmental milestones while Judith *weighed in* with the specific competency of smiling. Cara *weighed in* with the strategy of bright lipstick; Judith's family *weighed in* to adapt the strategy for Makai's father to put a bright sticker on his nose.

Be as equally open and honest about the professional's own strengths and needs as asked of the family (4.21). Early intervention is tailored to each family according to that particular family's priorities, strengths, and needs. Balancing power recognizes that EI professionals also bring needs as well as strengths to each FPP. Just like Judith's family was learning through the FPP, so was Cara and the other EI team members. Cara did not have previous experience with children with Makai's characteristics, which she honestly shared. Some professionals may feel uncomfortable admitting this, worried that this lack of knowledge in a specific area diminishes the professionals' expert power. However, Cara actually balanced the power by sharing what she did not know. Reciprocally, Judith did not see this as a deficit to the partnership, valuing Cara's knowledge of child development and intervention strategies. In fact, this helped balance the partnership as it made Judith "feel like equals" and "we're learning at the same pace."

Acknowledge and appreciate when families take the power they deserve and share the power they have (4.22). Frequently, balancing power is described as the professional sharing power with the family. However, families might share their power with professionals, turning the tables on the traditional family–professional roles, which represents another level of power balance. For example, recognizing the expert power Judith held regarding Makai's medical and developmental status, she initiated asking the professionals what questions they had about Makai. Judith also invited Cara to be a part of the conversation when making a decision about the DNR. Judith shared that "everyone involved in [Makai's] care should know what's going on . . . medically and how that affected us developmentally." Cara respected this opportunity—the power Judith shared with Cara—within her role of being available but without sharing her opinion.

Focus on the ultimate goal of family empowerment (4.23). One of the most powerful aspects of the above reflections is how clearly Judith's sense of self-efficacy and empowerment are described by both partnership members. Judith attributed some of this to her EI team and other professionals being "in my corner." Judith's family then felt confident to make medical and developmental decisions that were gratifying for her family. They felt comfortable because "the decisions made were ours" which resulted in "no regrets." That is early intervention success.

CONCLUSION: FAMILY AND PROFESSIONAL POWER PLAYERS

Both family members and EI professionals bring power to the family–professional partnership. The family brings the power of connection and interaction. The professional brings the power of developmental expertise, institution, and role. EI professionals use their power to foster the family's power. When the power of each member of the partnership is acknowledged and shared with equal force, the FPP propels forward in meeting their EI goals.

> **QUESTIONS FOR DAILY REFLECTION**
>
> 1. How did I spark each family's sense of empowerment?
> 2. How did I understand each family member's power to help me use my power?
> 3. How did I use my professional power to promote each family's power?
> 4. What were times I wondered if families felt powerful in the partnership? What did I do at those times?

CHAPTER 5

Partnership Collaboration, Communication, and Confidence

Sagarika Kosaraju

When a group of people work together in a collaborative relationship, sometimes the conversation can be awkward and stiff. Other times, it can feel uncomfortable, frustrating, and miserable. Then there are times when the conversation flows smoothly, each person contributes back and forth to the dialogue, and there is a synergistic effect in which both individuals walk away satisfied and with a new sense of meaning, growth, and connection (Aldridge, Kilgo, & Bruton, 2015; Aldridge, Kilgo, & Christensen, 2014; Viola, Olson, Reed, Jimenez, & Smith, 2015). It's this last type of conversation that EI professionals want to have with families. Through effective collaboration and communication, families will feel a sense of meaning, accomplishment, and confidence to support their child's development. The EI professional, Benny, reflects in this chapter on the "intricate dance" that can be cultivated by the professional, starting from the initial contact with a family and developing with each collaboration in which "together you will find one another's rhythm."

COLLABORATIVE DECISION MAKING IN EARLY INTERVENTION

A professional's approach—or attitude—coming into a relationship with a family often determines how successfully the partnership will unfold (Hansuvadha, 2009; Raver & Childress, 2014; Viola et al., 2015). In the EI research, attitudes frequently are found to be a barrier to partnering effectively with families (Coogle, Guerette, & Hanline, 2013; Hansuvadha, 2009; Lee, 2015; Strozier, Flores, Hinton, Shippen, & Taylor, 2016). Families can sense when a professional is skeptical of the information they are providing or is more focused on the legal procedures and the EI process than on the specific family circumstances (Hansuvadha, 2009; Lee, 2015; Strozier et al., 2016). However, a trusting relationship can slowly develop over time with the family when the professional uses the following approaches (Aldridge et al., 2015; Carroll, 2013; Coogle et al., 2013; Hansuvadha, 2009; Raver & Childress, 2014; Strozier et al., 2016):

- Is sensitive to the family's individual culture (e.g., religion, experiences with disability, household roles, or family stressors)
- Has a caring and positive outlook with the family
- Treats the family as equal partners
- Lets the family be the final decision maker

EI professionals are positive, respectful, and sensitive to the family's individual culture (5.1).

These approaches contribute to the professional's attitude toward the family, which in turn results in behaviors that empower the family to feel comfortable talking openly with the professional. These discussions lead to collaborative decisions that truly address the family's priorities (Raver & Childress, 2014; Viola et al., 2015). But when families and professionals do not feel free to express their opinions, interventions fall short. Approaching a collaborative relationship with a positive and nonjudgmental attitude toward the family helps start the partnership off on the right path (Coogle et al., 2013; Strozier et al., 2016). However, the professional also needs to prevent and address possible communication misunderstandings so collaboration continues to flow smoothly (Viola et al., 2015).

PREVENTING AND ADDRESSING COMMUNICATION MISUNDERSTANDINGS

Communication strengthens the collaborative partnership one interaction, or step, at a time (Raver & Childress, 2014). Both the professional and the family give (provide responses) and take (ask questions) in the reciprocal relationship (Lee, 2015; Viola et al., 2015). According to research (Aldridge et al., 2015; Al Khateeb et al., 2015; Carroll, 2013; Lee, 2015; Raver & Childress, 2014; Sass-Lehrer et al., 2016; Viola et al., 2015), ways to establish effective communication with families include the following:

- Address family communication needs and preferences
- Disagree respectfully
- Have a plan to resolve conflicts
- Be willing to compromise

On a practical level, the type of communication used depends on the family's individual needs and preferences, such as their primary language, interpretation requirements, and verbal and nonverbal traditions (Al Khateeb et al., 2015; Carroll, 2013; Evans, Feit, & Trent, 2015; Raver & Childress,

Partnership Collaboration, Communication, and Confidence   71

2014). Professionals need to keep in mind that each family may prefer a different form of communication, such as text messages, emails, video conferencing, or phone calls between home visits (Raver & Childress, 2014). EI professionals allow families to communicate honestly so that they may agree and disagree with the professional (5.2). If a family never disagrees with the professional, this may be an indication that the family does not feel comfortable expressing their true opinions.

When communicating with families, misunderstandings are inevitable and need to be addressed as soon as possible (Raver & Childress, 2014). Conflicts can be used as an avenue to explore the best possible solution for the child through a candid discussion (Jayaraman, Marvin, Knoche, & Bainter, 2015; Raver & Childress, 2014; Viola et al., 2015). Conversing in a calm voice with families, especially when discussing differences of opinion, can allow others to express their thoughts openly and without feeling threatened (Aldridge et al., 2014; Raver & Childress, 2014; Viola et al., 2015). Expectations for how to resolve conflicts can be outlined carefully during the IFSP meeting so the family–professional partnership knows how to navigate the discussion (Raver & Childress, 2014; Viola et al., 2015). For example, one FPP member may take the role of facilitator or each member may take turns to present their views during the meeting (Viola et al., 2015). Armed with the information from all team members, the family decides the resolution (Carroll, 2013; Viola et al., 2015).

Being willing to compromise and negotiate decisions shows that the professional is listening to the family and values their opinion (Aldridge et al., 2015; Carroll, 2013; Lee, 2015; Raver & Childress, 2014; Viola et al., 2015). EI professionals talk about misunderstandings openly and calmly to better comprehend the family's perspective (5.3). Compromising does not mean that professionals have to concede to all of the family's ideas or to potential injustices, such as instances of gender inequality, due to cultural backgrounds or experiences with disability (Aldridge et al., 2014). Professionals knowledgeable about cultural and historical traditions can work with the family to address these differences and help the family achieve their long-term goals for the child (Keilty, 2016; Aldridge et al., 2014). For example, a family may want a son to receive more services compared to a daughter due to their expectations that the daughter will not need to have a profession as an adult and will stay home to raise a family. The professional can discuss with the family how EI services will help the daughter learn to care for herself and her own family in the future.

EXPRESSING CONFIDENCE

Every successful family–professional interaction leads to the family expressing confidence and competence in supporting their child's development

(Raver & Childress, 2014). The professional spotlights the family's strengths and thoughtfully provides feedback to challenges (Carroll, 2013; Jayaraman et al., 2015; Sass-Lehrer et al., 2016). Family strengths are supported through praise or reminding families what they are already doing well (Al Khateeb et al., 2015; Evans et al., 2015; Sass-Lehrer et al., 2016). When a strategy may not be going as expected (i.e., not achieving immediate results), professionals assure families that the "just right" solution will be found over time (Aldridge et al., 2015). Overcoming challenges with the child can be seen by families as opportunities for personal growth (Carroll, 2013). EI professionals make sure each family feels more empowered and skilled (i.e., confident and competent) to support their child's development (5.4). Professionals and families can brainstorm to agree upon decisions collaboratively that work best for the child and family.

AGREED-UPON VERSUS RECOMMENDED DECISIONS

A critical component to FPP collaboration, communication, and confidence is ensuring that early intervention decisions are *agreed upon* by the family, as opposed to *recommended* by professionals. Recommended decisions are advice professionals give to families, whereas agreed-upon decisions are those in which professionals and families discuss together to reach a mutually acceptable resolution. EI professionals assess the context of priorities with families and brainstorm recommendations that can be integrated in family-established routines (5.5). Ultimately, professionals need to carefully talk to families during assessment, planning, and intervention to agree how best to support the child.

Assessment

Whether during the initial evaluation or continuous progress-monitoring, professionals gather information using open-ended questions to understand the child's medical history, previous development, strengths, and needs. Assessment of the setting and family's daily routines also brings context to any challenges in routine activities (Kellar-Guenther, Rosenberg, Block, & Robinson, 2014; R. A. McWilliam, 2012). Professionals use active listening by attending to the speaker's words, offering acknowledgement and compassion toward the meaning of the communication, and responding empathetically (Coogle et al., 2013; Lee, 2015; Raver & Childress, 2014). Instead of the professional *recommending* the intervention focus (e.g., priorities, outcomes, and strategies) from the child assessment data only, the professional provides her perspectives on the child's learning and development within the context of the family's priorities, outcomes, and strategies, also uncovered during the assessment process. This sets the stage for an *agreed-upon* intervention plan.

Planning

With guidance and recommendations from the professionals, the family decides which intervention strategies to implement (Sass-Lehrer et al., 2016). Professionals and the family are talking equally, generating ideas, and collectively deciding which strategies to try (Ridgley, Snyder, & McWilliam, 2014). Professionals should keep in mind possible disparities in learning theories when openly brainstorming recommendations (Aldridge et al., 2015; Yahya, 2015). For example, some immigrant families from Asian countries do not have experiences with play-based learning, and may prefer "homework" with rote memorization (Yahya, 2015). Professionals can share research about the benefits of play, and learn the reasons for the family's preference. The FPP might then integrate hands-on activities that can be implemented while seated at a table. In this way, professionals and families agree upon an intervention plan by working within families' beliefs as well as the developmental research (Sass-Lehrer et al., 2016; Yahya, 2015).

Intervention

Once a plan is determined, the family implements the intervention during the family's routine activities (Kellar-Guenther et al., 2014; R. A. McWilliam, 2012). The FPP can use first those routines the family is most comfortable with to implement new strategies (Sass-Lehrer et al., 2016). When providing constructive feedback while the family implements the strategies, the professional uses optimism instead of attributing struggles to family characteristics (Carroll, 2013; Jayaraman et al., 2015). Constructive feedback can also be done collaboratively by asking the family openly about their feelings of comfort and success with the strategy. Strategies frequently take some trial and error before they work well with children. After the family practices, the professional's comments focus on long-term results and encourage families to continue implementing the strategy when the professional is not present (Aldridge et al., 2015; Jayaraman et al., 2015; Kellar-Guenther et al., 2014; Sass-Lehrer et al., 2016). By providing this feedback and gathering feedback, the EI professional then knows he is leaving the family with strategies they agreed upon collectively. Professionals who collaborate and communicate more with families are focused on the family member supporting the child, instead of the professional supporting the child, and may lead to more strategy implementation by families between home visits (Kellar-Guenther et al., 2014).

In the following reflection, Jen, a mother whose family is supported by early intervention, describes her relationship with Benny, the EI professional, and the rest of her EI team. In particular, she explains how collaboration and communication with Benny transformed the team, created successful outcomes for Ryan, her son, and uplifted her confidence and competence to support Ryan's development.

FAMILY REFLECTION: JEN

[The concept of collaboration within the family-professional partnership] is one of the most important things in the EI practice. I was having trouble with some of the other therapists and it was because they were too busy [with the perspective] of the therapists and the patient. In this case [with Benny], it's really the therapist and the parent, the therapist and the child, the therapist-parent-child, and the parent and child altogether. That's why we have so much success. I remember Benny was the one that came in and did the evaluation with Ryan.... I could really see that he truly cared about Ryan and wanted to help. When it came time ... for developmental therapy, I said to our intake coordinator, "Benny has got to be our therapist."

When we first started, I was talking to a friend, and she was like "Oh, you're going to love therapy. The therapist comes and you get an hour to yourselves," but I want to be there.... I need to get tips, [and] I need to brainstorm with someone.... It's important to be able to work together, feel comfortable with each other and figure out what works best for that individual child. Not all kids learn the same way and we found that throughout the process ... you have to do what you have to do to make sure that your child is getting everything they need.

A lot of times therapists come in and their vibe is off.... We had a little bad luck with our speech therapist.... She was very much "by the book" and telling me, "No, this is how we have to do it." I would say, "No, this is not how 'we' do it. This isn't how he is ...," and it just ended up where after she would leave, my little guy was worse off. He was distraught and he was upset.

Whereas with Benny, we figured out that we had to let [Ryan] come to us and follow his lead rather than forcing him. Benny gave me great advice. We were joking because I love to go to Target or Walgreens. He said, "Imagine if any time I was with you, you said, 'Let's go to Target and Walgreens,' and I said no. What would happen? I wouldn't want to go to Target and Walgreens with you anymore." You know that's kind of the same thing as this [speech] therapist when she forces my child to do something. I'd see when she'd come in and see my little guy be standoffish and back up—that was the "aha!" moment for me when I was talking to Benny about it. At the time, we figured out there has to be a good relationship between therapists and the child.

Ultimately, we ended up switching therapists and finding the right one. It's important for parents to do what they think is best for their child and not be afraid to speak up. Because I had a teaching background, I felt a little bit ahead of the game where I'd know this isn't right.... I was like, "Why am I having so much success every time that Benny is here, but when this other one is here, we kind of have a lull." My little guy had a lot of lulls for a while.... Then we got the new speech therapist, and then definitely we saw like crazy great success. It's important for all members of our team to be in collaboration. Not just the one therapist, but all ... therapists [who] are working with that child.

Partnership Collaboration, Communication, and Confidence

The [occupational] therapist that ended up getting on board with us, she actually called Benny because I think she was worried about the evaluation and what Benny told me was, "I think she's worried because it's her job. She needs to do the progress report." I wanted her to know that I don't need immediate results. I just want slow and steady. It was very clear in all ... [the] meetings that you could see the relationship that Benny and I had and the relationship that Ryan and Benny had. So [the therapist] ended up calling [Benny] and started asking, "What evaluation are you doing? How are you doing it?" That was when Benny had talked to her and said, "This is kind of how we learn. We have to take a step back and let him come to you." I was just so glad he had that conversation with her. It was like every session that we had with the OT was great. Everyone got better and better. Ryan warmed up to her, then it was really great because we felt, "Okay, this is what you have to do."

... I was worried each time we had to find a new [speech] therapist. I felt so bad. I talked to Benny about it and we both agreed that at the end of the day, I have to do what I think and I know is right for Ryan. It can be very intimidating, especially for parents that don't know anything about early intervention or how a child learns. They just want to check with professionals. Our intake coordinator was awesome.... She really helped a lot by making sure that we got whom we needed and what's best for him.... The intake coordinator knew that Benny and I had the same relationship, so she got a referral from him. She knew that this person would be on board and have the same philosophy that Benny had. When we switched to the new speech therapist, she came, I filled her in, ... she walked in the door and it was like five seconds and my little guy was cooperating, doing what she wanted him to do. Just all working together. That's how we figured it out....

A lot of times when Benny would come over, I would get the impression that the sessions were really for me where I would just sit and talk to him.... He was always saying, "What would be the number one thing you want for Ryan right now? What would be the number one goal?" so I told him. As it came time to leave the park, Ryan would get really upset. It was very hard for him to get back in the stroller. What we started doing during the sessions was we would walk to the park. It was great because while we were walking there and back, Benny and I were able to talk and brainstorm.... We were talking about how well Ryan does at home, like when it's time to give him a bath, he never fights. Ryan knows that if the therapist is coming, he knows what to expect. We figured out he just needs to know. He needs a warning that we're going to be leaving soon. He'd be playing or running down the slide. We gave him a warning and also gave him a visual cue. We would pull the stroller up to the slide. We would point to the stroller and say, "One more time and we're going to go bye bye." That's when he learned. It was like the first day we did it and he got it! ... From then on, that's what we did and it worked. It worked great.... It's important that the therapist and parent have to talk. The parents should not be afraid to ask questions, be involved or even question the therapist. "Why are you doing it like that? Should we try it this way?" Because when your child doesn't have words, you need to be the voice for them.

... It goes back to that [a] kid's relationship with their parents is a lot different than with their teacher.... I think the relationship that the child has with the parent is the most important because they need to be comfortable to do what they need to do to learn and grow. We have a balcony that kind of overlooks the downstairs room. I noticed that when I would leave the room that Ryan was a little bit more cooperative and was more vocal. What we would do is I would go upstairs and watch from above so Ryan couldn't see me. I was able to still watch and learn and see different techniques that they were doing. The therapists were able to accomplish what they wanted to get accomplished.... If I was in the room and he didn't feel like doing something, he could come whine to me. When I was gone, he [didn't] do this.

We brainstormed a little bit, "What can I be doing more to stop that?" We quickly figured out that fortunately, Ryan responded really well to praise. Luckily, I was a cheerleader back in high school and so anytime he was doing something good that I liked I'd say, "Oh, Ryan that's such a great job! Yay!" and it motivated him to keep doing that.... It was a really big struggle for me and I [was] waiting for that one split-second that he wasn't whining and I said, "Oh great job! You're not whining!" Finding what he responded to well was really the key to see that success.

... It's important to find those little—even if there's the tiniest moment— to find those times where you can encourage and give them that praise that they need. I think positive encouragement is motivation for just, well, anybody. I felt like there were times ... like two steps forward, one step back. And as we worked through the process, I got more and more comfortable with how it was working and what was going on. You can just never give up!

PROFESSIONAL REFLECTION: BENNY

Establishing and maintaining a communication partnership is the foundation for creating a relationship with families that fosters true collaboration and breeds mutual confidence in each other's knowledge and abilities. Many years ago I established a profound belief that families of children with developmental delays and disabilities are very knowledgeable, competent, and dedicated to helping their children succeed in all aspects of their family life. This deeply held conviction is embodied in the manner that I, as an early interventionist, communicate with families as I begin to explore their priorities and work with them to develop strategies that can be applicable to their unique family life. It requires me to be very self-aware of the power of not only the questions that I ask families but also the manner in which I respond to their answers both verbally and nonverbally. With each question or response that I provide I have the opportunity to either strengthen or weaken the

Partnership Collaboration, Communication, and Confidence

family–professional partnership as well as the capacities of the individual caregiver that I am working with.

I am also very cognizant of the importance of supporting the whole family system. The role of the family is critical for the overall development of the child, so therefore I am often attuning to the family's individual needs at a given moment. In some cases they may need me to be empathetic to something they are feeling and need to talk about, other times they may be ready for me to problem-solve along with them a particular issue they need assistance with and we may reflect on the effectiveness of the strategies that we have chosen, and yet other times we may simply be "wondering" together to better understand their child. I equate this matching of the needs of the caregiver to learning an intricate dance with a new dance partner. You must first learn about each other as partners, each other's style of learning, each other's strengths and weaknesses, each other's pacing, [and] where each other's placement will be as you let each other go to turn each other around. It is then through this process that together you will find one another's rhythm. Once I am able to attune in this manner to a family, the end result is increased confidence and communication.

It is important to know that as I embark in this process along with a family it is not without me at times stumbling and making errors. . . . There are times that I may misinterpret the cues that the family has given me or I may have missed a cue altogether. It is these times in which I have to be comfortable being vulnerable and being OK with not having the correct answer for a family at a time. It is in those moments that I found that responding with humility and recognizing that my knowledge is always growing, that is most helpful in further establishing the trust we have in each other within this family–professional partnership.

The following is my reflection of a time in which I worked with Ryan's family using this concept. I began working with Ryan and his family when I had completed his initial evaluation to determine eligibility for EI services at 19 months of age. His mother was his primary caregiver and the person that I interacted with most when I came for my ongoing home visits. From the moment I met Ryan's mother, I could tell that she was very aware of her child's strengths. While asking her questions about her child's skills, she would share with me how he learned best and the strategies she used to maximize his engagement and interest in exploration. Through the context of our weekly home visits, I began to see Ryan through his mother's eyes so that I could get a better understanding of what she determined to be his areas of need and how I could support her in achieving the goals she and her husband had set for him.

I had stated in my initial home visit with her that our time together during these home visits were going to be a time for us to share with each other ideas about how to help Ryan continue to grow and develop. I expressed to her that she, as Ryan's mother, was the expert in how Ryan learns, what their day-to-day routines are like, and what he likes and dislikes. I further went on to let her know that her insight of Ryan is of great value to this process. I, on the other hand, bring knowledge about how children develop and various ways to support children when they are learning new skills. When we merge both her expertise with the knowledge I bring together, we then can create a support system that will help his development flourish. Finally, I stated that as we embark on this journey together I will have various ideas. Some of them will work and some will not. I also let her know that I am not a person who gets easily offended so I asked her to please feel comfortable telling me when a suggestion I give her is not working or is unreasonable for her family.

Over the course of our time together we had several moments in which we put this family-professional concept into practice. I remember a time in which Ryan's mother wanted to take a moment to speak with me about her experiences with the other professionals on our IFSP team. She expressed that sometimes she felt as though the other professionals on our team and her son were not matching up and that the visits would end up in him crying, for the most part due to him being stressed. I asked what that was like for her, and she stated that it was stressful for her as well as her son and that these visits oftentimes had lasting effects in which he would be more stressed throughout his day. We spent some time talking about the feelings that this would bring up in all of us and we attempted to wonder about what the other professionals may be feeling during these visits as well. After some time doing this, Ryan's mother began to express an interest in finding some potential solutions to this challenge that she was experiencing. I began by asking her if she had already spent some time thinking about how she might approach this and we discussed the various options she had considered. We then began to think about how these options may play out and considered some additional options as well. In the end, Ryan's mother and I agreed that the option she would like to try would be to schedule some co-visits together with myself and the other professionals on the team so that we could provide them with some opportunities to see Ryan in a different light and possibly open the discussion for exploring how we may still be able to challenge Ryan in different manners without him becoming so stressed. Upon trying this, we reflected together on how this worked and what elements she would like to continue to use in supporting her communication with the professionals on our team.

Another instance in which Ryan's mother and I put this family-professional concept into practice involved a time when she had a particular idea that she wanted to try out during our visit. Ryan's mother stated that she had noticed that Ryan had moments in which he did much better trying new things and engaging with others when she was not there. . . . This led her to the idea she wanted to try during this particular home visit. She wanted Ryan and me to try a particular activity that she and Ryan would do as part of their daily routine. This activity involved playing with Ryan while he sat in the bathtub. . . .

So what we ended up doing after discussing was have me go into the bathroom with her son while he was in the bathtub. She stated that he typically does well in this routine, and it lends itself to him being more talkative and engaging. She had in the bathtub his foam letters and a couple of books and toys set on the sink next to the bathtub. We had agreed to have her be right outside the door of the bathroom so that she could determine how her theory was working out. (Side note here: I had been totally uncomfortable with this idea as I typically always have the families present in my visit so that I can coach them through things. That being said, I had to make a quick judgment call. At the time I wanted to make sure that I validated what she was feeling and [did] not disregard her desire to try out something that she was thinking. So as I quickly did a gut and mind check, I decided that erring on the side of sustaining our collaborative relationship would trump my feelings and desire for "best practice" at that moment.) As we embarked on trying out her theory, there were times where her son would begin to become upset and she would say from outside the bathroom, "he wants his boat." Then on other occasions when he began to fuss she would say "he likes it when you turn on the sprayer for him so he can play with it," or "he wants you to read him the wheels on the bus bath book." In essence she began to coach me through how to support him in this routine. When we finished up and she came in to dry him off and then we sat and reflected on how the theory played out is when we discovered how attuned they were with each other and how that helps develop language at the developmental stage he was at then.

In each one of these instances Ryan's mother and I were able to fall back on the partnership we had created with each other when we first began working together. One that was based on trust, communication, [and] an understanding that each of us had expertise to share and a commitment to work collaboratively to contribute to the success of her son. You have to trust the process and the parents. Sometimes we learn things even when they don't go exactly according to plan. It takes time to get to this place when we begin in the profession and are often trained very differently in our preservice experiences. This takes much self-awareness, patience, and trust. But once you experience it, you will not do anything else.

LESSONS LEARNED: PARTNERSHIP COLLABORATION, COMMUNICATION, AND CONFIDENCE

Based on Jen and Benny's reflections, many lessons can be learned in collaboration, communication, and confidence from their personal experiences. Below is a list of actions professionals can use with families. Each one is not necessarily exclusive, but support and enhance one another. Professionals can use the following practices:

1. Build multiple trustworthy relationships
2. Tell families you do not get offended easily—*and mean it!*
3. Spend most of the visit time talking to the family to meet child, family, and parenting outcomes
4. Check in with the family about goodness of fit

Professionals can review these lessons before meeting a new family, as well as analyze if they are using these approaches when challenges arise with families. Benny demonstrated each one in numerous ways with Jen's family—in how he decided to approach the family—and Jen validated these efforts in her reflection. As Benny described, he understood that each interaction with Jen strengthened or weakened their relationship. He kept this edict in mind every time he initiated and responded to the family. Each of the lessons learned are further explored below:

Build Multiple Trustworthy Relationships (5.6)

Although the need for a trusting relationship with the family is discussed in EI research, Jen identified the need for *multiple* trustworthy relationships: (1) professional-child, (2) professional-family, (3) professional-family-child, and (4) family-child. EI professionals strive to ensure each family member is at ease and trusts the professional (5.6.1). Benny cultivated each of these relationships by taking time to understand Ryan and Jen's needs. For example, when he engaged with Ryan during visits, Benny observed that Ryan did better when he let Ryan come to him. With Benny's support, the other professional members of the FPP eventually replicated this approach. Frequent and consistent conversations among all team members helped the family and professionals stay up to date with Ryan's progress and successful methods to support him.

To develop a relationship with the family, Benny explicitly stated to Jen that she was "the expert on her child" and should advocate for Ryan. This message was supported by his deeply held beliefs that the family "is knowledgeable, competent, and dedicated to helping her child succeed in all aspects of their family's life." To support this view, Benny developed an open and trusting relationship with Jen. He comprehended "each other's style of learning, each other's strengths and weaknesses, and each other's pacing."

Benny also helped Jen understand Ryan's behavior better through the professional, family, and child relationship. For instance, Benny made a choice as a professional about how to respond to Jen when she decided she wanted to observe bath time from a distance. He wanted to honor her idea to "only" observe, despite feeling that it was not "best practice." By allowing Jen to watch his interaction with Ryan at a distance, she learned how to decrease Ryan's behaviors of whining and fussing with her while also seeing how well she already knows her son and what he's trying to communicate. Benny supported his relationship with Jen by trying her idea, modeling his positive relationship with Ryan, and improving Jen's relationship with Ryan. Jen was able to compare her own and Benny's responses to Ryan's behavior, which gave her more clarity and confidence about the issue they were trying to address.

Tell Families It's Not Personal (for the Professional) (5.7)

From the beginning of their relationship, Benny told Jen he does not get offended easily and she could openly disagree with him. It can be difficult for a professional not to take comments from a family personally, but by doing so, it gives families freedom to talk openly. If the professional gets upset or assigns blame when the family says a strategy is not working, then the family will not feel comfortable telling the professional how they really feel during home visits. EI professionals take comments from families objectively and respond supportively (5.7.1). Jen discussed several decisions she made for Ryan. The support she received from Benny and the intake coordinator gave her the space to try new ideas, fail at some of them without being criticized, and make successful decisions for her family.

Spend Most of the Visit Time Talking to the Family to Meet Child, Family, and Parenting Outcomes (5.8)

Jen described the home visits as being a time for her—to brainstorm with Benny any "struggles" that she was experiencing with Ryan throughout the week. Benny used the majority of home visit time to focus on Jen working with Ryan rather than Benny working with Ryan alone. Jen actively participated during the visits by establishing her goals at the beginning of the visit and discussing how to use visit time in a way that worked best for her. Although the home visits with Benny occurred weekly, Jen also felt comfortable contacting him throughout the week to discuss issues that may have occurred. EI professionals spend almost all intervention time interacting with those family members who will be implementing the strategies between visits (5.8.1).

Check In with the Family on Goodness of Fit (5.9)

Jen pointed out that she and Ryan felt good after the visits with Benny, and described feeling a "lull" or "distraught" after the visits with some of the other professionals. These feelings can be indicators that the collaboration is not going well for the family. EI professionals use asking as a key to finding a better fit for the family in the intervention process (5.9.1). From the beginning, Benny checked in with Jen about the progress of strategies and brainstormed new ideas with her when needed. Additionally, he openly told

Jen how he has "to be comfortable being vulnerable and being OK with not having the correct answer for a family." This honesty allows for both professionals and families to feel as though they can talk freely about their ideas and make mistakes.

The speech pathologist, who was eventually dismissed from the team, was not finding success with Ryan or Jen, and recommended strategies that were "by the book." The occupational therapist, on the other hand, reached out to Jen and Benny to find out how to improve her interactions with Ryan and Jen. The occupational therapist's openness to hearing other suggestions and trying them ultimately improved her success. In this way, the professional does not need to have all the answers for the family, but can research and collaborate with the family and other team members to find the best solutions for the individual family.

CONCLUSION: AN INTRICATE DANCE

As Benny reflects, "matching of the needs of the caregiver" is like "learning an intricate dance with a new dance partner." Jen and Benny exemplify the synergy that can occur in effective partnerships between families and professionals (Aldridge et al., 2015; Aldridge et al., 2014; Viola et al., 2015). Consistent, open, and flexible communication can develop trusting relationships with families and increase families' confidence and competence to support their young children. When this "intricate dance" is figured out, the partnership is mutually beneficial and rewarding for all team members, and most importantly, for the family and their young child.

QUESTIONS FOR DAILY REFLECTION

1. What was my attitude toward each family? Which attitudes were not so positive? How can I shift those attitudes?
2. How were decisions made with each family? What are my strengths in collaborative decision making? What areas do I need to enhance?
3. How are my relationships with each family member? How can I improve those that are less than optimal?
4. How much time did I spend interacting with adult family members? With which families do I need to increase the time spent?
5. How did the family feel during or after the visit? If I don't know, how can I find out? How can I further support each family's confidence and competence?

CHAPTER 6

The True Teaming Test

Bonnie Keilty

Is the family truly treated the same way as professional team members are treated . . . if not better?

The role of families as equal and full members of the EI team has been a longstanding condition of early intervention success (Aldridge et al., 2015; Cheatham & Santos, 2009; Lee, 2015; P. J. McWilliam, 2010; Raver & Childress, 2014; Turnbull et al., 2015). In fact, the Division for Early Childhood (DEC, 2014) explicitly begins many recommended practices—across assessment, planning, and intervention processes—with, "Practitioners work with the family to . . . " followed by the specific practice. The importance of teaming is summed up in the DEC Recommended Practice TC2:

> Practitioners and families work together as a team to systematically and regularly exchange expertise, knowledge, and information to build team capacity and jointly solve problems, plan, and implement interventions. (p. 14)

While few would argue with this recommended practice, actual implementation of this practice can be difficult. Teaming as a group of professionals is tough, with different personalities, perspectives, and time commitments. Creating multiple teams—one for each family supported—compounds the complexity of this task as each family brings its own experiences, expectations, and availability as a team member, as well as comfort interacting with support systems, such as EI programs and professionals (Beneke & Cheatham, 2016). This challenge can result in professionals—intentionally or unintentionally—abridging families' roles on the EI team. Turnbull and colleagues (2015) summarized the research on families' perceptions and experiences teaming with special education professionals:

- Some families were successfully included as team members while others were not.

- Some families felt their role as experts was minimized in favor of the professionals' expert contributions to the team.
- Some families felt they were bearing the brunt of leading the teaming process.

These findings suggest that families are not always fully contributing and equitable members of their EI team. Therefore, this chapter focuses on the "true teaming test," which results from answering the question that began this chapter: Is the family truly treated the same way as professional team members are treated . . . if not better? By exploring this question, EI professionals can reflect on their current practices that support families as true team members and identify ways to enhance their teaming practices.

This chapter is not intended to make EI professionals feel bad or judged about their past teaming behaviors, but to acknowledge how challenging this work can be and to identify practices that do and do not meet the true teaming test. As Aldridge and colleagues (2015) stated, "If [teaming with families] . . . seems easy to accomplish, then professional team members are not recognizing that they often wield power and reinforce inequitable relations as prominent team members" (p. 349). The power discussion in Chapter 4 has direct implications for teaming as the EI professional has the power to assure that families are indeed treated the same way as other team members . . . if not better. If the family is truly treated like professional team members, families are respected and appreciated for their particular "disciplinary" expertise, and family and professional team members comprise a unified team.

FAMILY AS A DISCIPLINARY EXPERT

Teams are formed under the assumption that no one team member, or even subgroup of team members, have the same skills or roles needed to get the job done. Instead, team members combine their diverse skills and take on different roles to accomplish their goals (Bruder, 2010; Carroll, 2013). In transdisciplinary teaming, professional disciplines share their specific knowledge and skills, transforming each other's competencies beyond traditional boundaries (Bruder, 2010; R. A. McWilliam, 2010a; Turnbull et al., 2015). Professionals respect, value, and assume competence in each team member's educational history and disciplinary expertise (Bruder, 2010; Shelden & Rush, 2010). They recognize the competencies brought from those experiences as positive contributions to the team. While utilizing and respecting the family's expertise and history may be implied in transdisciplinary teaming, how the professional team members work together to then partner with the family has been the main focus. To truly team with families, the family's "disciplinary" expertise—their special field or branch of knowledge—is incorporated and utilized just like that of other team members.

For families, their specialty is their lived history and expertise that comes from their previous and current experiences functioning as a family and parenting their child, which prepared them to contribute to the EI team. However, as identified previously, research found that some families feel their knowledge and experiences are considered secondary to the expertise brought by professional team members (Turnbull et al., 2015). This creates an inequity that hampers team development, just as if one professional team member conveyed that their disciplinary expertise was more important than that of another professional member (Beneke & Cheatham, 2016; P. J. McWilliam, 2010; Turnbull et al., 2015).

Respect for team members' expertise includes not only the knowledge and skills the team members bring but the manner in which that expertise was gained, through their education and previous experiences, that make them the authority of that expertise (Bruder, 2010). For families, however, research has found that, while families identified a hopefulness about the future for themselves and their child and personal growth from their unique parenting experience, professionals do not always see the experience of raising a child with disabilities as a strength, but instead consider it a hardship or a burden (Carroll, 2013; Lalvani, 2015). In the true teaming test, families' disciplinary expertise and the manner in which that expertise was gained—by parenting their child—is equally valued as those of the professional team members and seen as a resource for the team. This has several implications for EI practice, as discussed below.

Recognize what professional team members are learning from each family just like the reciprocal learning that occurs from other disciplinary professionals in transdisciplinary teaming (6.1), as opposed to seeing these as unidirectional interactions where the professional is the advice-giver and the family is the advice-receiver (Barrera et al., 2012; Beneke & Cheatham, 2016). Not only are professionals learning things about the particular family to utilize in their interventions with that family, they are also enhancing their professional repertoire about families, children, intervention strategies, and ways to partner with families in general. When professionals reflect on and articulate these family contributions, equity is strengthened as the family–professional partnership is seen as mutually beneficial and no team members feel they "owe" other team members (Barrera et al., 2012; Turnbull et al., 2015).

See each family-professional partnership as a separate team and take the time to develop that team (6.2), as opposed to seeing the EI professionals as the permanent team and the family as "added to" the team for their time in early intervention. All team members do the following to develop a well-running team:

- Agree on the goals and purpose of early intervention as well as the roles of each team member (P. J. McWilliam, 2010; Raver & Childress, 2014). Agreement moves beyond telling the family how early intervention works to exploring together the reasons behind how early intervention works.
- Value teamwork (Shelden & Rush, 2010, 2013). Team members make the time to work through and fully participate in team processes and then act on the team's decisions.
- Identify a team leader, perhaps the service coordinator, who assures team functioning (Bruder, 2010; Shelden & Rush, 2010). The leader checks in with each team member, especially the family, to make sure the *teaming*, in addition to the supports received, is working and that the family doesn't have to take on coordinating or leading the team.

View families as competent in their role, while supporting them in learning new competencies (6.3), just like all transdisciplinary team members support one another. Professionals support other professionals in learning disciplinary techniques by answering questions, modeling, and providing feedback while the other professional practices (Bruder, 2010). These are the same ways professionals "coach" families (Keilty, 2016) while acknowledging that families and professionals have different types of expertise. Professionals recognize the variability of strengths the family brings to early intervention and builds on those strengths just like professionals vary in the cross-disciplinary competencies depending on their previous experiences to acquire knowledge and skills in other domains. Additionally, families with less experience teaming (some families might have a lot of experience in or outside of early intervention) might need more support in how to team, just like professionals new to early intervention also might need more support in teaming practices.

Value and utilize family perceptions or ideas (6.4), as opposed to dismissing perceptions or ideas as invalid when different from professional contributions. Consider the following example: The EI professional provides supports in the child's early care classroom and sees him engaging in unwanted behaviors. When the professional discusses this concern with the child's father, he says that the child does not behave that way at home.

If another EI professional team member said this, would the EI professional dismiss the comment by assuming that the other professional team member does not place any demands on the child? Most likely not. Instead, in line with how other professional team members are treated, the EI professional recognizes and values the father's disciplinary authority and asks him for some examples of when limits are placed on the child, his reactions to those limits, and how his father helps him cope (Bruder, 2010).

Invite all eligible families to apply for opportunities to contribute to the field, such as serving on an EI committee or participating in a research project (6.5), as opposed to professionals serving as gatekeepers, selecting which families to invite based on what is going on in families' lives (e.g., new to early intervention, transitioning out of early intervention, intensity of services, severity of child's needs). The latter could reflect the perception that raising a child with developmental delays or disabilities is a hardship, or that families need to be protected. EI professionals do not make decisions about what other professional team members can "handle." In the true teaming test, EI professionals share opportunities so individual families can decide for themselves whether they want to participate (6.5.1).

When the family is truly appreciated for their disciplinary expertise, the FPP becomes a unified team where families are seen as equally contributing members of team decisions.

ALL OF US, NOT US AND THEM

Consider the following description of events that might happen when a developmental evaluation is over:

After the developmental evaluation, the assessors briefly meet in another room so they can agree on the results they want to present to the family. Or, another meeting is scheduled to "give the results" to the family after the professional team members get a chance to review and discuss among themselves.

Does this sound like true teaming behaviors? Would two professional team members from different disciplines suggest they meet or discuss the results prior to sharing with other professional team members from other disciplines? By excluding the family, EI professionals convey that there is an "us" as professionals that needs to portray a "united front," which means there's a "them" as the family. Instead, true teaming means "all of us" as professionals and family members, teaming together.

Professional team members might feel it's important to speak together before meeting with the family because the family may wonder why all professional team members aren't on the same page should points of disagreement arise. This is exactly the reason why families *should* be a part of these conversations to see why each professional is on the team—what each one contributes to the conversation. The family will see how consensus is built among team members and that they, as equal team members, can also share their own perspective. They will see that the team finds a way to commingle all of the perspectives together. And families will see that professionals do not have all the answers, but that the team, including the family, identifies potential solutions to try (see "Adopt a 'Figuring It Out Together' Perspective" later in this chapter). In other words, EI professionals need the family as much as the family needs the professionals.

Of course this does not mean that there aren't times when it makes sense for professional team members to meet without the family. There are certainly times the family meets with select team members without others, such as during home visits with solely the primary service provider. However, EI professionals ensure the family is involved whenever the early intervention team meets to come to consensus or make decisions, conveying that the family is truly appreciated for their disciplinary expertise (6.6) (Shelden & Rush, 2010). Instead of family contributions being less valued as suggested by the research (Turnbull et al., 2015), they are actually more important to team decision making.

...IF NOT BETTER

The previous sections have centered on the first part of the true teaming test—is the family truly treated the same way as professional team members are treated. This section now addresses the second part, that is, " . . . if not better."

As in all teaming relationships, each individual team member's characteristics are identified and appreciated. Therefore, treating the family the "same" does not mean *exactly* the same. Instead, EI professionals recognize that families are distinct from professionals—in their contributions to, investment in, and impact on the team and achieving team outcomes (6.7). Contributions result from the unique disciplinary expertise the family brings—of understanding family and child functioning and development. Investment comes from holding a dual role on the team, as team members and recipients of the specified outcomes resulting from the team's work. For each family then, it's very personal. It's about *their* child. It's about *their* family. It's why all the team members are working together—to enhance the capacity of the family. Impact returns to the power of the family as the greatest influencer of child development (see Chapter 4). Therefore, families are not the "same" as professional team members. Instead of a secondary position that is sometimes reported (Turnbull et al., 2015), EI professionals recognize that families actually hold an elevated position, where their perceptions of the purpose, goals, and approach are privileged over other team members. EI professionals can uphold this position by doing the following:

- Express an attitude of caring (see Chapter 3) (Blue-Banning, Summers, Frankland, Nelson, & Beegle, 2004; Coogle et al., 2013; P. J. McWilliam, 2010)
- Empathize with family concerns and everyday needs (Lee, 2015; P. J. McWilliam, 2010)
- Ask the family to share their thoughts and ideas first (P. J. McWilliam, 2010); give the family's thoughts and ideas the weight they deserve while honestly providing one's own thoughts and ideas (Doran, Mazur, & Llagas, 2012)

- Build communication skills to effectively convey thoughts and ideas in a sensitive but honest way; practice this when professional team members meet

FAMILY REFLECTION: TEAMING AS FAMILY

Michéle shares her experiences with her family's EI team and provides advice on how to truly team as a partnership.

In Hawaii, where we live, 'ohana is the center of life. 'Ohana means "family." This concept is deeply rooted in the culture and daily life. Families are bound together and members must cooperate and remember one another. Nobody gets left behind.

Our journey began during an ultrasound when [we were] given part of our daughter Anya's unique diagnosis. Knowing this crucial piece of information gave us a little time to process the diagnosis and prepare ourselves mentally and emotionally for the road ahead. This is a luxury some families don't get to experience when a diagnosis comes later in a child's life. As first-time parents and now armed with this unique diagnosis, what was our next step? We didn't know. The children's hospital jumped in the driver's seat and got us started on our road. They gave us printed materials, made referrals for all of the necessary medical specialists, provided information for a support group, and most importantly made the referral for early intervention services. Did I read those pamphlets? To be honest, at that time I didn't. Which ones were most important? I'm not sure, there were so many to go through, I was overwhelmed with information at that point. I was still consumed with processing the diagnosis and all the questions I still had, questions that will never be answered.

Soon after settling into our new life, we received the call to set up our first early intervention meeting, the evaluation. I have to admit, I was a bit nervous. My initial thought was, "There are people coming into our house from the state," and there was a wave of "what if" questions that immediately followed. I created more anxiety and worry that wasn't necessary. What I didn't understand at this point was they weren't there to critique us. They were there to educate and help us with understanding our unique child. I felt more at ease once we met each member of the team. We witnessed the intense desire each team member had with helping families.

When creating our first IFSP, the question was asked, "What are the goals you have for your daughter?" We looked at each other confused and [we] both thought, "These are the professionals; wouldn't they know what is developmentally appropriate for our child?" Each team member shared their wisdom within their discipline, and we shared our wisdom within ours.

From the beginning they included us as a member of the team. I was "that mom" who spent every waking free moment on the Internet researching. I had my stack of Post-it notes to ask the team members at the next appointment. No matter what ideas or questions I approached them with, even if it seemed out in left field, we were never judged or criticized. Together, we created realistic, achievable goals. The constant progress with Anya's development showed working together as a team can create positive results. With the progress came our set of challenges and hard times. No road is complete without them. During the difficult times, their positive and encouraging words kept us moving. Our team was always available, and if they weren't they would always get back to us timely. If there were gaps with services, they would provide us with tools and information to continue to enrich our knowledge. We were very fortunate to have their wisdom, philosophy, and training.

Throughout our journey, I've learned to be humble, not proud, and to ask for help when [I] need it. Question what you don't understand. Partnerships work when all individuals involved in a relationship can openly bring forth ideas, discuss those ideas, and make decisions that everyone can agree on. Partnerships are give-and-take relationships. For parents, the early intervention team is the individuals that will be in your lives for the beginning of your unique journey, providing essential support to your child and family. We created a lifelong partnership and bond with our early intervention 'ohana. They were there for us during the most important and challenging moments of our journey. This is a gift that can never be forgotten.

Looking back, I wouldn't change a thing about our family's approach. The one thing I would change, is worrying less about the small things and the things I can't change, and focusing on the things I can change.

PROFESSIONAL REFLECTION: TEAMING WITH DIFFERENT FAMILIES

Jamie, a physical therapist, reflects on the need to develop a team with each individual family. He starts by sharing his experiences with Michéle's family:

Providing EI services for a young child is truly a partnership between the child's family and the EI professionals. EI providers have the academic degrees to be "experts" in their individual specialty, but it is the family who will be providing the ongoing, hands on "therapy" for their child. EI providers are "coaches" who empower families to become developmental experts in their own right . . . their child's developmental expert. In order for a child to maximize his or her developmental potential, EI providers and parents work as partners in order to ensure [that] developmental strategies can be incorporated into the child's entire day, every day, rather than only the 1% of the time the therapist is present. If families don't agree with your plan of care, they are less likely to follow through with the strategies therapists provide, which will significantly impact the child's progress.

The True Teaming Test

As an EI physical therapist, my ideal situations are when I walk into a family's home for the first time, and there is instant chemistry. The child's parents are eager to learn and "will do whatever their baby needs." This was the case the first time I met Anya's family. I walked in for her initial developmental evaluation and saw this beautiful bright-red-haired baby with increased muscle tone and a cleft lip and palate. Her genetic diagnosis was so rare, there are no exact results in Google. The closest we found was another diagnosis with a deletion of one of the chromosomes involved with Anya's diagnosis. From the beginning, Anya's parents and her therapists were unsure of what to expect with Anya's development. As Anya's skills developed or new challenges arose, we adjusted as necessary to meet her individualized needs.

Anya's parents "hit the ground running." I looked at it as my, and my co-workers', job to educate Anya's parents regarding typical development, where Anya was currently functioning, and what we were working toward. Anya's parents were always very receptive to our suggestions but also added incredibly valuable insight about the time between our sessions. For example, her parents told us by what date she needed to be weaned off of the bottle to have her cleft lip repaired, and as a result, our therapy adjusted accordingly.

Anya was a feisty baby (and is now a feisty little girl ☺). She became very upset during activities to decrease her tendency to "arch" during tummy time and sitting. Michéle and I did a great deal of problem solving to find activities that provided the appropriate benefit and [that] Anya would tolerate. I may be an expert on motor development, but Michéle is an expert on Anya. I went into great detail educating Michéle on how babies typically move, how Anya was moving and why, and what the exercises were trying to accomplish. We gradually found ways to help Anya learn to move using more typical patterns, which helped her attain her motor milestones. This would not have happened as timely or with the [same] level of quality if Michéle and I didn't work together as a team to customize a plan and figure out what worked for Anya.

Throughout Anya's time in EI, the service providers and her parents maintained an honest and open relationship. This communication allowed us to continually make adjustments regarding her motor skills, feeding, communication, cognitive, and behavioral interventions as necessary and helped Anya reach her developmental potential.

While the collaboration for Anya was open and seamless, this is not always the case. When meeting families for the first time, I like to use the *Forrest Gump* line of "Meeting families is like a box of chocolates . . . you never know what you're going to get." Every parent has a different personality, and each family its own unique dynamic. As previously mentioned, Anya's parents "hit the ground running." They saw the situation and wanted to start moving forward immediately. Not all families respond in this way. EI providers may become frustrated for multiple reasons: lack of follow-through, lack of participation or initiative during sessions, difficulty keeping appointments, difficulty connecting with the families, [and so on]. . . . Many factors could contribute to how parents react to their child requiring "special services," including, but not limited to, personal, cultural, or emotional reasons. Each family is at a different place in accepting their child's unique needs, and EI providers must recognize and appreciate each parent's state of mind.

Most providers can't relate to the emotional impact when a parent is told [her] child has special needs and may be "different" from other children. One can only imagine the emotional whirlwind: worrying will their child ever be independent, will he be picked on or made fun of at school, can they afford the services, should I quit my job and stay home with him . . . the list goes on and on. A common frustration therapists experience is when they have strong suspicions a child may have a genetic disorder, but the parents will not undergo genetic testing. Clinically, knowing the diagnosis and learning any specific precautions needed is helpful. However, therapists can be met with resistance when they talk about genetic testing, even when brought up in the most sincere way. This exact situation occurred recently. Each time we attempted to subtly bring up genetic testing, we saw the mother's attention "check out" [and] a "wall" went up. She no longer engaged in the conversation.

My coworker later suggested, "Wow, she's in such denial!"

I responded, "I don't think so. She's just not ready."

To clarify, I said, "Emotionally, she's not ready to hear the results. She sees there's a difference between her son and the other children. . . . She's just not emotionally ready to handle hearing this may be permanent. Once a diagnosis is given, it becomes 'real.' . . . Until then, she can hope, 'maybe he'll catch up' and will be 'normal.'"

As difficult as it is, we need to try to put ourselves in the shoes of each family. Just as I tell students and families I work with, "If you know *why* someone is doing something, it makes it much easier to remain calm." I typically use this to understand children when they refuse food or tantrum, but it holds with adults. If we, as clinicians, can understand *why* parents are reacting the way they are, it makes it much easier for us to remain calm and focus on helping them work toward achieving their goals. If we're able to "meet parents where they are emotionally" and not push our own viewpoint, we have a much better chance of establishing a cooperative partnership.

Recently, I found myself a victim of my own predeterminations before I even met a family. After the evaluation, we lost contact with the family. Their phones had been turned off by the carrier. The family contacted our program after more than a month and said the child had lice. Services were put on hold and, once again, we lost contact with the family. It became frustrating. We wondered, "Were they not interested in services? That's okay, but please tell us." It was, again, more than a month before the family initiated contact asking to proceed with therapy services.

In the past, when there was this level of difficulty [beginning services], when the families often canceled or "no showed" frequently, the parents often weren't active participants during sessions or in carrying over strategies. My thoughts at this time were, "I'm supposed to see her weekly? It's going to be one of those cases . . . "

I let my past experiences influence my initial mindset, but I *could not have been more wrong*! Yes, this family does not have a working phone, but they are amazingly efficient with email. After her evaluation, her family took the occupational therapist's initial recommendations and bought a chair for their daughter to sit in while eating and playing. As a result, her sitting balance improved significantly between her evaluation and her first therapy session. Every time I walk into their home, the family is excited to tell me what new skills their daughter has learned and are eager to learn "what is next." Recently, the child's sitting posture began to be compromised, as she was significantly leaning to one side. In discussing possible ways to help her, her parents listened with full attention. When I came back, the child's sitting posture improved dramatically. Her parents implemented every strategy discussed, and they made sure the grandparents were also performing the strategies.

In what I first thought was going to be a challenging case, I am now a part of another "ideal situation," just like with Anya. This was a huge wake-up call for me: Never prejudge a situation and always keep an open mind. We don't know what families are experiencing. We don't know why they aren't returning our calls. We don't know how they are feeling . . . until we ask them. Once we learn what each family's priorities are and address those priorities, we will have a great, cooperative partnership. When service providers and parents are open and on the same page, babies benefit.

LESSONS LEARNED: THE TRUE TEAMING TEST

Michéle and Jamie's reflections illustrate the true teaming practices described above. The FPP demonstrated mutual respect for each team member's disciplinary expertise. Michéle valued the "knowledge, philosophy, and training" of the professional team members, and Jamie noted the family as the "child's developmental expert" and how they contributed "valuable insights . . . [about] the time between sessions." Michéle and Jamie described how they united as a team to create agreed-upon IFSP goals, understood and appreciated how they would collaborate to address those goals (as described by Jamie), and how professionals "never judged or criticized" Michéle or her family (as described by Michéle). Jamie emphasized the " . . . if not better" component of the true teaming test by acknowledging that the professional may not fully understand the "emotional impact" of having a child with a disability (P. J. McWilliam, 2010). Michéle and Jamie provide additional lessons learned for achieving the true teaming test below.

Adopt a "Figuring It Out Together" Perspective (6.8)

In this team, the uncertainty around the defining characteristics of Anya's diagnosis provided the opportunity for all team members to come together as a team to *figure out* the best intervention approach. However, even when a diagnosis is known, there is great variability in its presentation and impact on participation and learning for a particular child in a particular family. So the same "figuring it out together" perspective can be used with all families. By Jamie bravely acknowledging he doesn't have all the answers—and it is brave for professionals to let go of the security of the professional stance of "expert" (as also described in Chapter 4's family and professional reflections)—the professional team members approached their work as learners, just as much as the family team members did. Traditional boundaries of expert-provider and novice-receiver no longer apply. In turn, this approach benefited the EI program too, as seen in Michéle's reflection. While there were "gaps with services," Michéle accepted this problem as one for the "true team" to *figure out* and collaboratively identified ways to continue to meet the team's goals despite this roadblock.

Scaffold Families to Achieve Their Teaming Roles (6.9)

Let's further explore Michéle's family wondering why they were expected to identify the IFSP goals at their first IFSP meeting. Of course it is the role of the family to identify the goals that are important to them. However, families might be uncertain of what to say or how to respond to the overarching question, "What outcomes do you want to address in early intervention?" Without guidance, a family might draw from professional recommendations on eligibility evaluation reports, which potentially do not reflect the family's actual goals. They might, as Michéle wondered, cede this role to the professionals' expertise (i.e., "power"—see Chapter 4). Instead, professionals scaffold families uncovering their goals using various approaches, including open-ended questioning, Routines-Based Interview, and ecomapping (see Chapter 7 for one process) (Jung, 2010; Keilty, 2016; R. A. McWilliam, 2010b).

This does not mean, however, that families take on professionals' roles. Sometimes, professionals lose their "voice" in an effort to be family-centered, deferring to the family's desires (Dunst & Espe-Sherwindt, 2016). For example, what if, once Michéle's family identified their IFSP goals, the family was then asked to identify the developmental steps and strategies to best achieve the goals? This is the expertise brought by professional team members. It is the reason the family came to early intervention in the first place. EI professionals support families in identifying specific outcomes and contribute their expertise to determining developmental steps and intervention strategies to scaffold families in the consensus decision-making process (6.9.1).

Identify, Relate, and Apply the Family's Perception of a Team and Teaming (6.10)

Each family–professional team will look and act different from other FPPs just as every professional team would, based on the characteristics of its team members. Of course professional preferences and characteristics certainly contribute to the team's approach. As both the primary team member and the recipient of the team's efforts (see the section ". . . If Not Better" earlier in this chapter), it is the family's previous experiences and expectations that guide the development of and approach to teaming.

As with engagement, each family will begin early intervention at a different place in terms of readiness to team. Jamie described Michéle's family as ready to "hit the ground running." Other families may be unaccustomed to teaming. Each family's openness to teaming can be influenced by their cultural expectations for partnering with professionals, their opinion of the benefits of teaming, and their previous experiences with formal support systems (Beneke & Cheatham, 2016; Edwards, 2016; Hanson & Espinosa, 2016). These past experiences could be with medical and EI systems as parents, with educational systems as students or parents of older children, and other social systems as an individual or family. To support the team development process, EI professionals appreciate the influence of the family's perspectives and previous experiences on their readiness to team, and guide the family as they build teaming skills within their comfort zone (6.10.1) (Aubin & Mortenson, 2015; Hanson & Espinosa, 2016).

From Michéle's reflection we learned her perception of her EI team as extended *ohana*, or family. This perception most likely developed over time, within the intimacy that occurs within home visits (Fialka, 2001). However, other families may keep the partnership friendly, but never choose to see the team as personal as Michéle described her team. EI professionals recognize that families will differ in how they view professional team members and are flexible and fluid in how each team interacts according to the parameters set by the individual family (6.10.2).

Assume Positive Intent, With or Without the "Why" (6.11)

From his "aha!" moment, Jamie identified the old adage "Before you criticize, walk a mile in their shoes." Behaviors make sense—or are "functional" as Jamie put it in positive behavior supports terms—when the family's reasons behind those behaviors are appreciated. This appreciation may result from the professional's own similar experiences—the professional has walked a mile in the same or comparable shoes—or when the professional learns the reasons for why the family is acting a certain way. In the latter, the professional's hypotheses of "why" are replaced with the authentic reasons. For example, similar to the genetic testing example in Jamie's reflection, Lalvani (2015) found that, while a sample of special educators interpreted the family's opposition to labeling their children as being "in denial," the families in the study explained they were not in denial, but were concerned that labeling would stigmatize and negatively impact their child. While professional team members might have good reasons for a preferred approach—like Jamie identified, "to learn if there are any specific precautions"—family team members may also have good reasons for preferring a different approach. EI professionals create a safe space and initiate a discussion with the family to understand the reasons for their actions, replacing the hypothesized "why" with the actual reason (6.11.1). EI professionals can explain the spirit in which this conversation is raised, namely, to understand, to avoid making families feel defensive (R. A. McWilliam et al., 2011).

While putting oneself in another's shoes is easier when the reasons behind the family's behaviors are known, professionals may not always know the reason. Families may not want to share or may not be fully clear themselves as to why. Or, as in Jamie's situation, families may simply be unavailable to share their reasons. Regardless of the situation, professionals can take a strengths-based perspective and assume there's a good reason for the family's actions. Over time, the reason may become apparent, such as when the family contacted the program to explain the child had lice and their phone didn't work. Or the family may change their minds. For example, the other family in Jamie's reflection may one day choose to have the genetic test should they come to see the value. However, professionals should not pressure the family or assume that one day they will change their mind. EI professionals recognize that the reason they assigned to a family's actions is not necessarily accurate, and they reframe any deficit-based assumptions into strengths, whether or not that strength is known (6.11.2) (Barrera et al., 2012).

Question Denial (6.12)

The term *denial* is often used in early intervention to describe someone disagreeing with another or not acting as another would want (Cheatham & Santos, 2009; Gallagher, Fialka, Rhodes, & Arceneaux, 2002). Denial is frequently used by professionals when talking about families, as illustrated in Jamie's reflection (Hansuvadha, 2009; Lalvani, 2015). In fact, attributing denial to families of children with disabilities is so common that, in Lalvani's (2015) study, families who refuted that they were in denial acknowledged that other families might, in fact, be in denial. Professionals can question whether a family is in denial by asking the following questions:

- *Do the family's behaviors really suggest denial?* In Jamie's reflection, he distinguished the family as "not ready to hear the results" from being in denial. The family is enrolled in early intervention and partnering with the professional team members. This suggests that the family recognizes—and therefore is not "in denial" about—the child's unique developmental needs and the role of early intervention.
- *Is it about facts or a difference of opinion?* In Jamie's reflection, the family was not disagreeing with the *results* of the genetic test, which would have, presumably, provided objective evidence of a diagnosis. The family was disagreeing with the *need* for the test to inform intervention and future development. Applying the true teaming test of equal weight *if not better* given to the family's disciplinary expertise, professionals can uncover and discuss with the family their reasons (i.e., "the why") for rejecting the recommendation for testing, and come to consensus as to next steps for intervention.

A difference of opinion can also occur when discussing future developmental expectations for the child. Professionals sometimes identify that families' expectations for their child's learning and development are unrealistic (Gallagher et al., 2002; Hansuvadha, 2009; Lalvani, 2015); however, Gallagher and colleagues (2002) explained:

> No one can accurately know or precisely predict what children with disabilities will accomplish or become in their future. Still, some professionals characterize parents as "in denial" when they think the parents do not accept their child's disabilities and limitations. (p. 11)

EI professionals avoid attributing families' behaviors as denial and seek to understand each family's perspectives (6.12.1).

CONCLUSION: THE TRUE TEAMING TEST

Regarding families as equal and fully contributing members of the EI team is a long-established recommended practice. The principles and practices of transdisciplinary teaming can be used in developing a team that respects and utilizes the family's disciplinary expertise just like professionals' expertise. At the same time, EI professionals privilege the family as both team member and recipient of the team's work. EI professionals can use the true teaming test to determine if families are treated the same way professional team members are treated . . . if not better.

> **QUESTIONS FOR DAILY REFLECTION**
>
> 1. What did I learn from each family that enhanced my competencies to support all families?
> 2. How did I treat families "better" than professional team members? Where might I enhance my practice in this area?
> 3. What actions did I use to convey and practice within the true teaming test? What else could I do?
> 4. How did I support families in teaming and building their competencies? How could I further support them?

CHAPTER 7

Going Deeper to Truly Understand

Bonnie Keilty

> I recognize that the power of intervention does not lie simply with the family learning strategies to meet a child's needs. Knowledge of strategies does not produce a sense of competence or confidence in their role as parent. It is when a parent couples their knowledge and understanding of their child and their routine activities with a vision that the parent ends up developing confidence that they are capable in their role as parent. Watching a parent (caregiver) become both competent and confident in their role as parent brings deep satisfaction to me as an interventionist.
>
> —Erin, occupational therapist

The partnership concepts explored in the previous chapters are most likely somewhat familiar to the reader. These concepts are frequently discussed in the literature, during professional development, and—while perhaps different terminology is used—espoused in expected early intervention practices. Hopefully, those chapters further deepened readers' understanding of each family–professional partnership concept. This chapter also discusses "going deeper," but deeper into the family and how they think about the ways they help their child learn and develop in everyday life. Therefore, as Erin identified in the quote above, the focus is not about families learning and then following through with specific intervention strategies between visits, but garnering each family's strengths to build their confidence and competence in their parenting role of helping their child learn and develop as they envisioned (Dunst et al., 2007; Trivette et al., 2010).

STRENGTHS-BASED INTERVENTIONS THROUGH FAMILIES' FUNDS OF KNOWLEDGE

As identified in Chapter 4, strengths-based interventions (SBIs) are the cornerstone of early intervention. SBIs utilize the family's *funds of knowledge* (González, Moll, & Amanti, 2005)—their already existing understanding, interactions, and resources related to child learning and development—to foster new competencies in the family and the child to meet their parenting goals (Dunst at al., 2007; Khetani et al., 2013; LaForme Fiss et al., 2013; Palisano, Chiarello, King, Novak, Stoner, & Fiss, 2012; Rush & Shelden, 2011; Trivette et al., 2010). The funds of knowledge concept recognizes that all "people are competent, they have knowledge, and their life experiences have given them that knowledge" (González et al., 2005, pp. ix–x). Unpacking this definition, EI professionals can do the following in practice:

1. Work from the assumption that families have, and are *already using*, specific approaches to help their child learn (i.e., competent)
2. Recognize that these approaches are based on the family's *understanding* of child development and reflect the family's goals for their child's learning (i.e., knowledge)
3. Appreciate *how* these approaches and understanding came to be as a reflection of the individual family's thought processes, problem-solving approaches, and outside resources that contribute to helping their child learn (i.e., experiences)

When EI professionals uncover all these components of the family's funds of knowledge—how the family thinks about and helps their child learn—they can then draw from and purposely apply these strengths to planning and implementing developmental supports (Di Santo, Timmons, & Pelletier, 2016; Moll, 2015; Reyes, Da Silva Iddings, & Feller, 2016). While the funds of knowledge concept is used more in early childhood general education, strengths-based intervention, and particularly family strengths, are more commonly used in early intervention.

Families in early intervention access their strengths to understand and help their child learn and participate in everyday life. In a study to uncover EI families' strengths around how they help their child learn, the researchers found the following results (Keilty & Galvin, 2006):

1. Families used a variety of approaches to help their child learn across different routine activities, and added and eliminated different approaches as the child grew and developed.
2. Families had very clear and conscious reasons for using the approaches—those they created on their own and those supported by EI professionals—based on their knowledge of their child, the goals they had for their child, and the characteristics of the routine activities.

Therefore, families do not come to early intervention absent of ways to promote child learning. Families come with a history of thinking about, interacting with, and seeking to understand and help their child learn within their family's cultural values and ways of functioning. To design SBIs, EI professionals go deeper to uncover, appreciate, and apply the family's understanding, perceptions, and approaches to helping their child learn (i.e., strengths) in the design and implementation of interventions.

GOING DEEPER: STRATEGIES WITHIN ROUTINE ACTIVITIES

Early intervention has long been rooted within the routine activities that comprise the family's natural environment. The practices described in Chapter 2 are essential to understanding how the family goes about their day; those routine activities reflect the family's overarching strengths and what's important to the family (i.e., priorities). The child's learning and development is examined *within* these routine activities, and strategies that families can use to enhance their child's learning and participation are identified and embedded into particular routine activities.

"Going deeper" moves beyond the characteristics of the routine activity and how the child participates to the more complex, reciprocal influence of the child and the approaches to support child learning and development occurring within those routine activities. These approaches are the *strategies* the family uses to promote child learning, individualized as needed to his or her unique developmental characteristics. "Going deeper" does not negate the importance of practicing in routine activities, but instead EI professionals explicitly mine the learning strategies occurring within routine activities and the family's perceptions behind those strategies to understand the strengths the family brings to early intervention (7.1) (see Figure 7.1). To go deeper, EI professionals uncover strengths and plan interventions based on those strengths.

Figure 7.1. The Relationship of Learning Strategies to Routine Activities

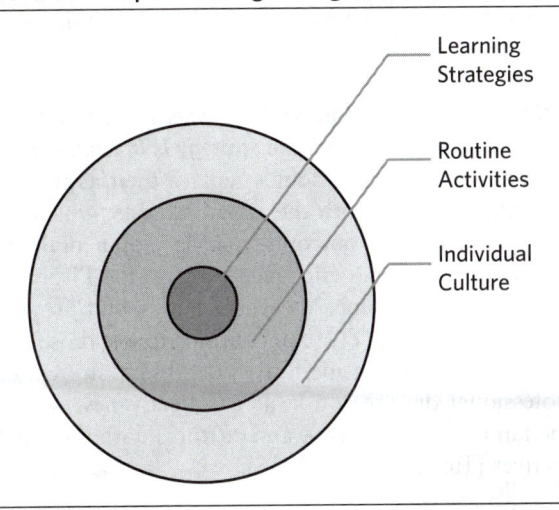

Uncovering Family Strengths in Helping Their Child Learn (7.2)

What are the family's specific strengths in helping their child learn? The answer to this question focuses intervention on enhancing what the family is already doing to help their child learn and target areas where assistance is needed, all attuned to the family's goals and perceptions of how early intervention can help. The author of this book has developed an assessment-to-intervention approach, called *Family Strengths in Child Learning* (FamSCL), based on the research described earlier (Keilty & Galvin, 2006, 2014). While this approach is being tested for its utility in creating SBIs, EI professionals can use the following questions that were a part of the initial research and included in the FamSCL to understand the family's strengths, developmental strategies used, and perceptions of those strategies.

What learning strategies does the family use, in which routine activities? These learning strategies may be specific to the child's unique learning characteristics or generally used to promote child learning and development. Learning strategies include modifications to the physical environment (Chiarello, Palisano, Bartlett, & Westcott, 2011), responsive interactions, and specific instructional strategies. With this knowledge, EI professionals avoid recommending strategies the family is already using and identify potential strategies that can further enhance what the family is already doing. For example, the research cited above found that families often used a variety of strategies that were sensitive to the child's developmental characteristics, one aspect of responsive caregiving (Keilty & Galvin, 2006). However, families infrequently used contingent responsiveness, another important aspect of responsive caregiving. If an EI professional sees that this holds true for a particular family, interventions can acknowledge the family's strength in using sensitivity strategies and focus on identifying and embedding contingent responsiveness strategies.

What does the family hope the child will learn when the family uses the strategy, and how effective does the family think the strategy is in helping the child learn? Through these questions, EI professionals replace their assumptions of why a family uses specific strategies with the actual reasons, which results in uncovering the family's underlying outcomes and developmental priorities. The family's perception of a strategy's effectiveness helps the EI professional pinpoint where and how to intervene. When the family and professional agree on a strategy's effectiveness, the FPP can continue to use those strategies that are effective and concentrate on ineffective or absent strategies. When the family and professional disagree on strategy effectiveness, the professional understands the family's point of view and partners with the family to merge the two perspectives (Turnbull et al., 2015).

How did the family figure out to use that particular strategy? EI professionals uncover the family's thought process, problem-solving approaches, and other resources in helping their child learn, which results in data on how the family thinks about child development and how early intervention can best help. For example, in the Keilty and Galvin (2006) study, while families appreciated EI professional input on designing learning strategies, they varied in the types of support desired, ranging from prescribed strategies taught to them in prescribed ways to general information that the family then tailored to their own family. The support desired depended on the characteristics of the strategy as well as the family. Knowing the family's support preference for a particular strategy, EI professionals can tailor their coaching support to that preference.

Figure 7.2 illustrates how these questions align to the unpacked funds of knowledge definition referenced earlier. Taking the time to explore the individual family's funds of knowledge results in the data needed to intervene according to the family's strengths and needs.

Just like child strengths and needs are understood through authentic assessment methods, rich information about the family's strengths and needs related to helping their child learn can be gathered through the authentic methods of naturalistic observations and discussions with the family. And just like assessing children, each methodology contributes specific data necessary for a complete picture of child *and* learning supports. For example, if EI professionals only ask families what they do to help their child learn, most families may find it hard to respond (Di Santo et al., 2016; Keilty & Galvin, 2006). They might think what they are doing is nothing out of the ordinary but simply what parents do. They might not even know they are using specific learning strategies. Therefore, observing what's happening is important. EI professionals become a "fly on the wall" to see what families do to promote their child's learning and development in everyday life (7.2.1). Conducting

Figure 7.2. Alignment of FamSCL Questions to Funds of Knowledge Definition

Strategy Questions	Funds of Knowledge Definition
• What learning strategies does the family use, in what routine activities?	• Families have and are already using specific approaches to help their child learn (i.e., competent)
• What does the family hope the child will learn when the family uses the strategy? How effective does the family think the strategy is in helping the child learn?	• Approaches used are based on the family's understanding of child development and reflect the family's goals for their child's learning (i.e., knowledge)
• How did the family figure out to use the particular strategy?	• The approaches used reflect the family's problem-solving approaches and outside resources (i.e., experiences)

observations and coming to conclusions about what is observed is very common practice with young children. However, this observation is about the *adults*—with harder-to-suppose motives, intentions, and expected results than children. Therefore, discussions with families about what is observed are needed. For example, an EI professional may think a family whose child has visual impairments uses the strategy of running the child's finger over braille when reading a book to prepare the child to read braille. When discussing this strategy with a family, the family might identify reading readiness is indeed a long term goal, but the strategy was particularly used to give the child the same experience other children have when they read books—to engage with the book through touch (Keilty & Galvin, 2006). EI professionals combine observations and discussions to truly understand the breadth of learning strategies used and why they are used so the family–professional partnership can then plan strengths-based interventions (7.2.2).

Plan Interventions Based on Family Strengths (7.3)

Planning interventions that understand and enhance family strengths requires interpreting the assessment data gathered through the questions above, along with authentic child data, into a clear picture of the transactional influence of the child, family strategies, and family perceptions of their child and intervention priorities (Sameroff & Fiese, 2000a, 200b). With this information, EI professionals design and implement interventions that are fully aligned to the family, including their parenting style, how they think about their child's learning and development, and what kind of help they want from early intervention (7.3.1). The FamSCL guides professionals to then plan interventions at the routine-activity and learning-strategy levels (Keilty & Galvin, 2014):

- **Intervene at the routine activity level** by checking in on, but leaving alone, the routine activities where the family has it all figured out and focusing on those routine activities where strategies the family uses are less effective.
- **Intervene at the learning strategy level** by reinforcing the well-designed, developmentally promotive strategies the family already uses, tweak the ones that are almost there, and collaborate to find new or substitute strategies when the current ones are ineffective.

Erin, the professional who contributes her reflections in this chapter, suggested:

> This is a wonderful time to compare routines that are going well with routines that are challenging. Analyzing with the family what strategies work well, under what circumstances, and why deepens their capacity for reflection and problem solving. It also promotes their confidence for such tasks.

The resulting plan is attuned to (1) the family's underlying desired outcomes for their child's learning, (2) the family's strengths and identified needs related to helping their child learn, (3) the specific times of the day when support can be most helpful, and (4) the kinds of support desired.

By looking deeply at the learning strategies families use, early intervention can maximize its impact on positive child outcomes by focusing on families' effective use of learning strategies tailored to the child's learning strengths and needs (Innocenti et al., 2013; Khetani et al., 2013; Kong & Carta, 2013; Raab et al., 2013; Smyth et al., 2014; Trivette et al., 2013). By creating strategies and providing supports tailored to the family, EI professionals won't have to worry about families "following through" with strategies recommended during EI visits. Instead, families simply will utilize those learning strategies, because the strategies are primarily those they are already using, in ways they always expected to parent. Figure 7.3 outlines how focusing on the learning strategies families use amends interventions focused on routine activities to go just one step deeper.

Figure 7.3. Amending Early Intervention Practices from Focusing on Routine Activities to Focusing on Strategies

Focus on Routine Activity	Focus on Strategy
• Similar strategies are recommended for most families when working within the same routine activities.	• Strategies are tailored to each family based on the strategies the family is already using and the reasons the family uses those strategies.
• Professional learns families' perceptions of routine activities and how the child participates in those routine activities.	• Professional learns about the strategies families already use and the motivations behind those strategies within routine activities.
• Family learns new strategies agreed upon by the FPP.	• Family learns about strategies they are already using and new strategies as needed.
• Family is the expert on their family; professional is the expert on interventions. They pool their expertise.	• Professional and family are both experts on interventions. Professional uses expertise to boost what the family is already doing.
• The focus of the intervention visit is to ensure the family will follow through with agreed-upon strategies between visits.	• The focus of the intervention visit is to check in on the strategies that already work, tweak those requiring modification and, if needed, add new strategies so the family can continue doing what they are already doing, with increased effectiveness, between visits.

PROFESSIONAL REFLECTION: ERIN DISCUSSES GOING DEEPER

Erin, an occupational therapist, shared her written reflections about going deeper with a particular family:

Parents are most confident and competent in their role as caregiver when we seek to understand their knowledge and perspective about their child's needs. From there, we develop a plan of care that utilizes the parent's valuable insight and understanding of meaningful ways to include interventions into the family's daily routines. Parents most consistently implement strategies and utilize supports when they actively contribute to the problem-solving and planning process.

I work with a family, originally from India, whose ... child was born with many medical conditions. When I arrived on the scene, ... he was nonverbal, nonambulatory, made little eye contact, was fed through a tube, and everything seemed to upset him. ... The child's mother excelled at meeting and managing the child's many medical needs. She was first concerned with her son's ability to take food by mouth and was upset that she had not yet found a way to consistently or effectively calm her child. She wanted him to be able to enjoy the people and world around him.

Our first step was ... reading her son's emotional signs and ... understanding his sensory needs. We focused on developing therapeutic strategies into activities that were already taking place and meaningful to her. The mother learned to modify traditional Indian massage and breathing practices. She learned to determine the speed of movement and amount of pressure that was "just right" and calming. The mother began to see and feel how her emotional state and her movements could allow her to connect with her son. She began to successfully read, adjust to, and effectively support her son's organization.

During this time ... [I] provided information about self-regulation, and reflective questions expanded the mother's ability to see the world from her son's perspective. The mother was able to identify and select other daily activities that could be modified to become calming opportunities. Bath time was transformed from a task to be survived daily to a time of calm, connection, learning, and independence. The reflective process also served to help the mother understand why she acted in certain ways. For example, the mother reported that in her native culture it is common to make sure children get what they need. It is accepted that children will sometimes resist or avoid some things that are good for them. This realization, coupled with an understanding of her son's severe sensory-processing needs, led the mother to see how she met her son's medical needs but struggled to support his ability to calm. The mother was relieved to have this emotional conflict resolved.

As her son's ability to interact with the environment and people and food improved, we needed a plan to progress from his being tube fed alone and often while in bed to a new and more functional arrangement. The mother also took steps to learn to introduce foods in ways that were least invasive. We role-played to help her gain the child's perspective and used parent perspective to set new mealtime participation goals. For example, I fed her and she was asked to give me signals to control the speed/pace of food presentation and the amount of food on the spoon so that eating was comfortable for her. We repeat this process as one phase ends and another begins, such as when the child met goals, when the development of the little sister allowed mealtimes and play interactions to change, and as the parent's desire for family functioning changes.

I began to see that there were definite stages to our process. Initially, I provided new knowledge (sensory) and helped the parent understand the child's perspective. By doing so, she could begin to recognize his signals/communication attempts, which allowed her to respond in respectful and loving ways to his sensory/emotional wants and needs. I realized that the child's medical issues and basic survival had been the parent's priority and during that phase things had simply been done to him to ensure he survived. The downside to that was that it did not encourage self-regulation and he developed strong aversions to many routines/activities. [The mother] was very changed when she began to understand the child' perspective. I could see she had a deep need not to just meet his medical needs, but also . . . to fulfill his emotional needs. We began to explore the role of a child in a family and how that looked in her mind. She immediately began considering how mealtimes would look, [as well as] . . . outings, play, and cuddle/social times. As the family grew we revisited the idea of siblings learning from one another. The mother was able to express the things she thought the older child could learn from the baby as the baby progressed through different phases. [This resulted from the mother seeing that the child imitated the younger sister reaching up to be picked up.] The mother selected excellent learning times throughout the day. When summer arrived and [the child] was home from school, the mother wished to develop a daily schedule that could meet the needs of the whole family. This included planning outside time early in the morning to beat the heat, mealtimes with both children and/or the whole family eating together, naps, activity/learning times, as well as whole-family and social times. All routines took into account the child's sensory and developmental needs, schedule, and the family's vision for themselves. I realized that these parents, by providing variety, structure, and a deeper understanding of why specific strategies worked, had become not therapists but simply loving parents who knew their children with a great degree of depth.

I was delighted to watch the family transition from survival to appreciating the child's perspective; to understanding and meeting not just basic needs, but fostering learning and social interaction that was meaningful and special to their family. They became a family with dreams and with the strategies and skills to attain those dreams.

FAMILY REFLECTIONS: WHY GOING DEEPER WORKED

The family Erin partnered with in her reflection above shared with Erin their thoughts on how going deeper was essential to effective early intervention:

"Traditional therapy" did not work with my child because his needs were so unique. Because of all his surgeries (8 in first 2 years) and doctor appointments (170 in first 2 years), our family and our son [were] always in a state of recovery and transition. The therapists wanted to help him move, but he could not hear and did not attend to people. We had a very difficult time trying to consistently do the therapists' recommended activities because the activities did not address his sensory needs (which we didn't know about) or help him attend to people. We could not tell the difference between OT [occupational therapy] and PT [physical therapy]. . . . Before [the cochlear implants were placed, my child] . . . was always in his own world, without giving visual attention or interaction with others. [Erin] helped me see that my energy and the sensory input I provide to my son greatly affects his ability to focus and attend to me. The right therapist is very important, but in the beginning I was so overwhelmed I did not know if the therapists were a good fit. I just knew we were doing all we could to meet the medical needs of our child.

[Erin] took the time to help me see the things that I already knew and taught me new things. In this way, I can increase my child's success, even on a bad day. For example, [my son] was very sick and not wanting to drink from his sippy cup. [Erin] had mentioned [earlier] that he was ready to drink from an open cup. So I realized that if I remove the top, the sippy cup would become an open cup. When I did this, my child was intrigued by the newness and was excited to sip many times. I can think of many more alternatives to turn a bad time into a good time.

[Erin] continually helps me think of what is coming next. Once she describes what possibilities are coming next, then I start thinking about how I can introduce this new activity or idea to my child. I usually know what strategies or routines or times of day . . . might work best, and if my idea fails, we develop new plans together. For example, he has begun looking at me when he wants something, usually his implants so that he can hear. [Erin] observed that he was doing this consistently and asked, "How can you encourage him to help you or to put them on himself?" I knew right away that I would put on the right implant and then talk to him and encourage him to help me place the earpiece behind his ear and to put on the left implant.

[Erin] understands where the family is at with many things, [such as] . . . living circumstances, changes in family like a new baby or traveling. . . . [Erin] sees the good in each session and points it out to the parent, which lifts the family's spirits and encourages us. I used to say, "He's not eating, or he's only eating one bite." [Now] . . . he can eat again! There's a way he can do it.

Sometimes he wants what he wants. It's not always what I want. After his throat surgery I'd totally lost hope that he'd ever eat by mouth again. Working with [Erin] . . . I now know that [my son] can learn from big changes and challenges (e.g., traveling, moving, exploring, and eating by mouth). I hope to keep trying new things so that he can continue to grow.

I was helped greatly at times when I was frustrated or unsuccessful. We also work well when anticipating new chalienges [such as the] family trip to India, anticipating safety concerns in the new home like gates for stairs, [and] setting up rooms/spaces in the new house for specific purposes. [Erin] . . . changed her visit times to match my child's needs. . . . We progress at a rate that is consistent and good. [Erin] . . . always asks me, "Of the things we tried today, what's realistic to focus on next week?" She helps me think of our schedule and then I decide what makes sense to work on. This way I am not as likely to get overwhelmed.

LESSONS LEARNED: GOING DEEPER

These reflections demonstrate how uncovering the family's funds of knowledge influences how well interventions fit the family. The initial interventions (i.e., mobility) were disconnected from the family's main priorities around their child's medical needs and the developmental priorities of hearing and attending. Upon joining the EI team, Erin took the time to establish a partnership by learning about the family, which resulted in a better fit. The following lessons learned are illustrated in the FPP's reflections.

Understand First, Then Plan Intervention (7.4)

Just as one would not create interventions without child assessment data, understanding the family's strengths precedes intervention planning. This process does not delay intervention, but can be considered a part of intervention as both FPP members learn about the family's already existing strengths in helping their child learn. Erin identified and supported the family in seeing "things [they] already know" and built interventions from there. Returning to Figure 7.1, Erin described the process she used to understand the family's strengths in their individual culture (outer layer) and routine activities (middle layer):

> Families set the priorities of intervention by identifying times that they would like to see go more smoothly or by sharing their "dream" for what a given routine/situation might look like. The parents are encouraged to remember their own meaningful and memorable childhood experiences and family traditions that they would like their child to experience too.

And then digging deeper to understand the family's routine activities (middle layer) and learning strategies (inner layer) occurring within, Erin added:

> When partnering with parents I first seek to come alongside them so that I can see how well they already understand and meet the needs of their child. I identify the strengths and interests that are unique to each parent/family member and their current role/responsibilities with the child, as well as the learning needs of each.

By understanding first, the family's competence, knowledge, and experiences guide intervention design (Di Santo et al., 2016; Moll, 2015). The FPP identified strategies the family is already using that are effective. At the beginning of intervention, the family's strategies that worked well addressed the child's medical needs. The FPP also identified strategies that, with modifications, could be effective to help the child's self-regulation. These strategies included the Indian massage and breathing practices. These strategies—those already successful and those somewhat successful and then modified—became an important part of the intervention plan. All members of the FPP know that the strategies will be used because the family is already using them. The number of new strategies the FPP needs to identify and embed are then limited to those areas not addressed by the already existing strategies.

See Through the Eyes of the Family (7.5)

As identified earlier, understanding the family's funds of knowledge includes seeing the situation from the family's perspective rather than making assumptions as to why it occurs as it does. Erin came to understand that the bath time routine occurred the way it did, not because the family did not recognize the child's regulatory needs or know that bath time could be better. But instead because, in the family's culture, "children will sometimes resist or avoid some things that are good for them." The family may know that the way (i.e., strategies used) the child is bathing is not as effective as it could be. And Erin recognized this as an "emotional conflict." The family did not have another strategy to meet both the child's bathing and regulatory needs. By replacing potentially erroneous assumptions with the actual reasons behind the approaches (i.e., strategies) the family uses, the FPP was able to identify ways to make bath time a calm experience while also meeting the expectation that the child needs to take a bath.

Use the Process to Build a Mutually Trusting Relationship (7.6)

The process of understanding first to see through the eyes of the family is not only to gather knowledge about the family, but also to create a "relationship

Going Deeper to Truly Understand

of trust" (González et al., 2005, preface). In uncovering families' strengths, EI professionals trust families can think about and utilize learning strategies that promote child development because families already are thinking about and using strategies (7.6.1). As Erin identified:

> It is in this process that we, as clinicians, come to trust the parents' knowledge and understanding of the factors that affect their child's learning/acquisition of new skills and the child's responses to interventions. It is also the process by which the clinician begins to trust the family's reasoning to both refine existing strategies and develop new ones.

Families learn to trust EI professionals as the professional conveys sincere interest and assumption of competence in the family, and utilizes her or his professional expertise to build upon, instead of replace, the family's strengths. The family in the reflection discussed the perceived trust in the above family–professional partnership:

> It is based on trust. I understand what [Erin] . . . says is true because of her experience and training. When two brains think [together], it is more productive. Trust allows me to honestly share problems and challenges. We work together to make my life easier. [Erin] . . . must be patient and willing to answer all of my questions. Also, the parent has the responsibility to honestly try the strategies generated with the therapist.

As discussed in Chapter 3, trust is built over time. The process of digging deeper provides that foundation. The process, however, does not come without its challenges. EI professionals must ask questions in ways that convey curiosity and illustrate reflection on the family's responses (i.e., what does this information contribute to intervention?) without the family feeling tested. In other words, the EI professional does not question the reason behind using a strategy, but questions to understand the reason. The EI professional then applies the responses in intervention design to demonstrate that the questions were asked in good faith to assure a goodness of fit between the family and intervention (R. A. McWilliam et al., 2011). Erin described this as

> a process of collaboration that includes reflective questions [and] reasoning, [with] therapist-shared knowledge . . . and at times good old-fashioned trial and error.

Trusting in each other's strengths allows the FPP to problem-solve together.

Provide the "Just Right" Support (7.7)

In an email, Erin described a specific moment when the family was sharing their reflections:

> At one point, the mother said, "You tell me to do things and I trust you, so I do them." I responded, "I wonder if you realize how little I tell you to do and how usually I rely on your knowledge of the child to determine how to introduce the next thing." This led us to the realization that I often show her what's next and she is really the one who figures out the "how." Making this realization together served to deepen the trust and respect in our relationship.

This quote sums up the reciprocal relationship in this family–professional partnership during intervention visits. Based on her professional expertise, Erin provides anticipatory guidance (Dworkin, 2000) or, as the family described it, "to think of what is coming next." The family uses this knowledge by "thinking about how I can introduce this new activity or idea to my child" based on the family's expertise of "knowing what strategies or routines or times of day that might work best." The FPP merges their strengths to design and test out potential strategies, as seen in the example with the cochlear implants. While the FPP primarily used this approach, there were times when more direct support was used, such as with the role-playing of eating. The approach used changed as the FPP determined how much support was needed for particular situations (Keilty & Galvin, 2006). By working from the way this particular family can best utilize EI supports, which may be different for other families, Erin is providing not only just the right amount of support for the child based on the child's strengths and needs, but also just the right amount of support for the family. This builds the family's confidence to extrapolate strategies to other developmental concerns, such as how the family used Erin's anticipatory guidance to solve the sippy cup dilemma, as well as begin to anticipate herself, such as identifying how the younger sister's emerging abilities (i.e., lifting arms to be picked up) can encourage the older child to do the same.

Watch Out for the Early Childhood Challenge (7.8)

EI professionals come to the family–professional partnership with a toolbox of strategies. Usually, EI professionals can quickly and easily identify multiple ways to address specific developmental concerns and promote learning in specific routine activities. However, strategies common to early childhood may or may not fit a particular family. The challenge for EI professionals is to move away from typical "early childhood" expectations and strategies common for particular routine activities, and instead allow for interventions to differ with each family based on their understanding of the family and their individual strengths (Reyes et al., 2016). In reflecting over time about this FPP, Erin identified times of transition as when she may share relied-upon "early childhood" strategies rather than ensure that the strategies truly fit the family:

> I think, as I grow in my ability to read situations and as my experience grows, I will be able to navigate transition times more fluidly. Sometimes it took several visits to come up with a workable plan [during transitions such as] when the family moved, went on vacation, had company, and needed to set up the house. I now have a better understanding of what to expect and in the future can do better to plan ahead with the [family].

When there is a shift in any part of the intervention process, such as when the family's life circumstances change, new child goals are identified, or new team members join, EI professionals might feel pressure to respond with the strategies in their toolbox without considering whether or how those strategies fit the particular family. Or, if time is tight due to limited duration, number, or frequency of intervention visits, EI professionals might try to provide as many strategies as possible in the shortest amount of time. These situations are opportunities for EI professionals to step back and reflect on whether the EI professional *recommended* a particular strategy to the family or the FPP *together arrived at* a particular strategy based on the family's current strengths and priorities. If it's the former, EI professionals dig deeper with the family.

CONCLUSION: GOING DEEPER

This chapter explored how going deeper provides rich information to mold supports to fit the particular family. The family is then more confident as interventions are built from the competencies they already bring to their child's learning, augmented by strategy modifications and additions that increase effectiveness. When there truly is a goodness of fit, "interventions" are ongoing, with the EI professional supporting the family as the family supports the child. The success of the family–professional partnership in this chapter is illustrated in the family's desire to keep in touch with the professional about those between-visit moments:

> I would like to begin texting the therapist to share moments of success! It is so wonderful to share with her when things go well. Also, if I text her, I will not forget to share the successes with her.

> **QUESTIONS FOR DAILY REFLECTION**
>
> 1. What strategies was each family using between intervention visits? How do I know they were using those strategies?
> 2. Why was each family using each of the strategies identified in #1? How do I know that's the reason? How effective does each family think each strategy is?
> 3. How did I emphasize strategies the family is currently using as important ways to promote child learning? What other currently used strategies were modified? How did the family respond to our discussion about these strategies?
> 4. What new strategies did we agree upon? How did the family respond to these strategies?
> 5. How did I convey trust in the family through the conversation? Did this process increase the family's trust in me? How do I know?

Conclusion

Reflections and Lessons Learned on the Unique Partnership Culture

Bonnie Keilty

This book delved into seven concepts that illustrate what it takes for successful family–professional partnerships. These concepts reveal the complexity of building and sustaining positive relationships with families. It is sophisticated work to identify the different ways of knowing and apply the EI evidence base and recommended practices within the family's cultural lens (Chapters 1 and 2). Engaging families and assuring equity of power in the partnership is not easy (Chapters 3 and 4). The nuances involved in effectively communicating and collaborating to truly team requires skillful negotiation of one's words, actions, and perceptions (Chapters 5 and 6). And finally, the EI field continues to evolve, digging further into and better fitting family life so that what families do to help their child learn and develop feels natural and validating (Chapter 7). This evolution expects EI professionals to be comfortable and competent in deeply analyzing and applying the conclusions drawn within intervention design and implementation in partnership with the family.

In order to achieve these FPP concepts, EI professionals are required to be thoughtful about what these concepts mean and, subsequently, what EI professionals need to do to achieve them. EI professionals take care to avoid translating the concepts to fit what the professional is already doing, and acknowledge that, in some ways, their practices need to shift to truly implement all of the concepts with each and every family supported. To assist readers in this journey, this Conclusion revisits the three themes for successful early intervention described in the Introduction.

FAMILY–PROFESSIONAL PARTNERSHIP AS THE ESSENTIAL RELATIONSHIP IN EARLY INTERVENTION

Each chapter identified specific practices and lessons learned for the individual partnership concept that, taken all together, illustrate the kind of family–professional partnership essential for successful early intervention. Across partnership concepts, some common themes emerged, each of which could promote successful FPPs when applied and impede FPPs when they are missing. These themes are described below.

The family's individual culture is the culture of the family–professional partnership. EI professionals understand the family's culture to inform the focus of early intervention (i.e., priorities and outcomes) as well as how early intervention occurs (i.e., types of supports, intensity, suggested strategies). Reciprocally, EI professionals look at their own practices and the potential influences of their own biases and perceptions in the ways EI professionals create and sustain each partnership. For example, in a sample of occupational therapists, one study found that implementing family-centered care was more difficult when families' characteristics were different from the professionals' characteristics, most particularly in linguistic, cultural, and income diversity, as well as when families had multiple needs (Fingerhut et al., 2013). These findings illustrate the effort necessary to wholly implement the partnership concepts, especially when that means reconciling seemingly unrelated perceptions of parenting, priorities, and the role of early intervention. EI professionals explore their understanding of culture and how cultural differences can influence family and professional behaviors and, therefore, the family–professional partnership (8.1).

Attitudes and beliefs matter. The practices described in this book seem difficult to implement unless one truly believes in them. For example, does the EI professional really believe that families can take or dismiss EI professionals' advice? Does the EI professional really think of families as partners as opposed to service receivers? EI professionals identify the values, beliefs, and attitudes inherent in the partnership concepts and lessons learned; explore the alignment to their own values, beliefs, and attitudes; and seek resources to reframe any misalignment (8.2).

Family–professional partnerships are dynamic. Just as families shift their parenting as their child grows and develops or when they learn new information and strategies, FPPs shift over time. Families acquire more information about their child, the systems in which they participate, and how partnerships work. Families acquire new skills, such as observing and interpreting their child's behaviors and generalizing strategies to other situations, as well as become more skilled in partnering with professionals. Transition points—developmental shifts of the child as well as changes in systems and supports such as leaving early intervention—influence what supports families desire. EI professionals continually seek feedback to understand and respond to changes in families' expectations for, and interactions within, the family–professional partnership (8.3).

Conclusion

Early intervention fits in families; families perceive early intervention as family. The reciprocal nature of this theme is shared in many of the family reflections. EI professionals are identified as "family" due to either the friendly, informal approach to supports provided or the closeness of the relationship built from the intimacy of the work (Fialka, 2001). As such, EI professionals recognize and respect the vulnerability and trust that families have invested in the family–professional partnership (8.4).

We're in this together. The notion of partnership conveys the reciprocal nature that no one partnership member has all the answers; partnership success depends on each other's contributions. Early intervention is about hypothesizing and testing. It's about taking educated guesses of what could potentially work (through assessment processes) and then trying it out (through intervention) to see whether or not it actually works (through progress monitoring). EI professionals actively build partnerships with families to jointly carry out the data-based process of questioning, strategizing, and analyzing (8.5).

Accurate perceptions matter. Interpreting adult (i.e., family member) behaviors is difficult. Another adult can assign erroneous assumptions of why one may be acting a certain way. EI professionals avoid assumptions by explicitly asking families for their thoughts, opinions, perceptions, and reasoning, and then accept the family's response as truthful (8.6).

The practices described in the previous chapters are specific ways these themes are applied. Taken together, they illustrate the essential relationship that occurs with each individual family.

INDIVIDUALIZATION AS THE ESSENTIAL INGREDIENT OF FAMILY–PROFESSIONAL PARTNERSHIPS

Family–professional partnerships are transactional. Each partnership member influences the other. All the chapters discussed the uniqueness of each family and each child. While Chapter 1 discussed the importance of working within early intervention's evidence base, it should be noted that, of course, not every professional is exactly the same. Each professional has her or his own interaction style and approach to partnership development, even when responsively partnering. Additionally, each partnership is unique in the priorities and outcomes to be met, as well as ways of collaborating. EI professionals recognize and embrace the uniqueness of each family–professional partnership; what "worked" for one family may or may not work for another (8.7).

What makes the "right" match for a successful family–professional partnership? The ingredients for a successful partnership are complex and includes the interactional characteristics of all FPP members, as well as the support desires of the family. Further research is needed to determine the combination of family and professional variables, including the kinds of supports desired, to help guide the field to proactively identify the best family–professional fit (R. A. McWilliam, 2015). In the meantime, EI professionals recognize that there are those times, albeit infrequent, when an FPP is simply not a good fit, regardless of how well the professional engages in partnership practices. EI professionals appreciate and facilitate, rather than become discouraged, when a change in partnership members is needed (8.8).

Early intervention is all about the individual—the individual child, the individual family, and the individual FPP. EI professionals reflect on how the partnership concepts work best within each individual family–professional partnership (8.9).

REFLECTION AS THE ESSENTIAL COMPONENT OF PROFESSIONAL GROWTH AND DEVELOPMENT

Professional reflection is professional development. The idea of "reflect[ing] productively" (Santagata & Angelici, 2010; p. 340) moves reflection from thought (i.e., What do I think about what happened?) to action (i.e., What should I continue to do and do differently based on what happened?). Professionals who "practice" as a developmental process recognize that, through reflection and action, they can continually enhance their practices. EI professionals can reflect on and then respond to what the family–professional partnership concepts look like in each early intervention process and with each family (8.10).

What the partnership concepts look like in each early intervention process. EI professionals consider ways to utilize the partnership concepts as they proceed through each component of the early intervention process. They determine how best to build and sustain relationships with families to determine (1) how and what to assess in order to (2) plan the IFSP so that (3) interventions are created, implemented, and evaluated in ways that meet each of the partnership concepts.

What the partnership concepts look like in each family. EI professionals reflect on their interactions with families and identify what made them successful and what is impeding the partnership. The reflection questions at the end of each chapter and the practices listed in Appendix B provide a framework for such reflection. This reflection does not occur broadly with all families as a sum total, but for each and every family, recognizing that some partnership concepts are more easily implemented with certain families.

Conclusion

While this can be difficult to acknowledge, without honestly looking at how one interacts with each family, one cannot change those practices that impede partnership development and work.

Even when EI professionals think the partnership is working, they look to the family's behavior to discover whether or not a partnership is indeed working. They reflect on what the family does (i.e., their behaviors), what they say (i.e., statements made), and how they act (i.e., their "vibe"). EI professionals can reflect on what feels right and what feels odd or unexpected. This is not to assign blame on the family or to pardon the EI professional from figuring out how to remedy any partnership barriers. In fact, the responsibility lies with the EI professional to do just that. EI professionals reflect on the family's reaction to the partnership as evidence that something is not working. When this occurs, the EI professional speaks with the family about his or her observations (i.e., confirming the accuracy of perceptions) and, together, they identify ways to address any issues. At these times, EI professionals may solicit support from other partnership members, peer mentors, reflective supervisors, or, when the issue lies in systems design, program administrators.

SYSTEMS INFLUENCERS

The family–professional partnership is influenced by the EI system in which supports are provided. This system can facilitate or impede FPPs (Keilty, 2013). In *The Early Intervention Guidebook for Families and Professionals: Partnering for Success* (Keilty, 2016), three systems factors were identified as necessary in order for professionals to implement EI-recommended practices—flexibility, professional expertise, and feedback procedures (Halle, Metz, & Martinez-Beck, 2013). These same factors can impact FPPs. EI system administrators can review policies and procedures, including funding mechanisms, to ensure that EI professionals have the flexibility necessary to respond to partnership needs. Sustained, sophisticated professional development resulting in effective implementation of FPP practices and attitudes—either as a prerequisite for EI practice or mandated once practicing—is expected, assessed, and verified. EI administrators also need to hear from those "on the ground"—families and professionals who are experiencing early intervention every day as it is currently implemented. The unintentional impact of specific policies and procedures are assessed and understood. Feedback from families and practitioners are respected and utilized to enact change that facilitates successful FPPs.

Federal EI legislation (Individuals with Disabilities Education Act [IDEA], 2004) and regulations (Early Intervention Program, 2011) affect the family–professional partnership from a more distal position. As Dunst (2012) pointed out, there is a discrepancy between recommended EI practices, with a focus on developmental promotion and family support, and EI policy, which focuses on services. These policies, of course, guide how states structure (and fund) EI systems and how programs implement (and fund) professional supports. Some states have indeed found ways to, by and large, implement current recommended practices in spite of this disconnect. However, as research and recommended practices further acknowledge and steer early intervention work toward more complex and sophisticated practice, the gap between policy and research will be increasingly difficult to bridge. Work at the federal level requires significant shifts in both the legislation and regulations to align with the current evidence base and make room for shifting practices as the field learns from research new ways to enhance EI practice.

THE PRIVILEGE OF EARLY INTERVENTION PRACTICE

Each FPP is an essential relationship that requires nurturing. The reflections of the families and professionals who contributed to this book demonstrate their commitment to developing and sustaining their FPP. It is an honor that they shared their stories and insights with the authors and readers alike. It reminds everyone that early intervention is truly a privilege—a privilege to join families on their parenting journey and to watch their child grow and their family develop so that, at the end of early intervention, the family is ready to navigate their next parenting adventure.

APPENDIX A

Examples That Illustrate and Do Not Fully Illustrate Each Partnership Concept

Below are examples that illustrate the nuances differentiating practices that truly apply the partnership concepts from those that do not.

1. Differentiate Ways of Knowing and Professional Decisions

A father identifies discomfort in the intervention strategy of putting his leg in front of the child's crawling path so the child can crawl over it.

Illustrates: The EI professional discusses with the father why the strategy feels uncomfortable. Once identifying the father does not want to hamper his child's movements, the FPP agrees to use the same strategy, but with pillows in the child's path instead. That way, the father is not impeding the child's movements and, instead, he helps the child as she climbs over the pillows.

Does not illustrate: The EI professional abandons the strategy without discussion, uncertain of a commensurate strategy; or the EI professional tries to convince the father to use the strategy as it will help the child in the long run.

2. Appreciate Family Priorities, Values, and Culture

The EI professional was always quite impressed with the twins' ability to self-regulate, especially falling asleep on their own. The mother discusses readying the twins for the arrival of the family's new baby.

Illustrates: The mother shares that she and her spouse will continue the strategy developed in EI of rocking the twins to sleep before bedtime and having them fall asleep on their own at nap time. That way, the twins get a chance to regulate their sleep/wake cycles while still having that close, quiet parent–child time.

Does not illustrate: The mother shares how nice it will be to be able to rock this baby to sleep, since she never was able to figure out how to do that with two babies at once. The EI professional was surprised to hear this as it was not previously discussed.

3. Build Family Engagement

The EI professional struggles with the family's engagement during the EI visit, but has consistent "conversations" with the family via text between visits.

Illustrates: The EI professional uses texting as opportunities to reinforce the importance of family engagement during the visits, identify the family's priorities, and set a plan for the visit that fits the family's priorities and depends on the family's active participation.

Does not illustrate: The EI professional is satisfied that the family is at least texting for now and continues the visits with limited family engagement.

4. Recognize the Power of Partnership Members

The FPP has been using sign language as a way to develop the child's communication, which has been quite effective. The family identifies a few more nuanced words/signs that they want the child to learn. The EI professional thinks that it might be difficult for the child to differentiate when to use these new words/signs from when to use similar words/signs he already knows.

Illustrates: The EI professional acknowledges the family's interest and notes what they need to consider in helping him learn the difference between the words/signs. If the family is still interested in teaching those words, together the FPP identifies times throughout the day when each word/sign can be used and ways to support the child in initiating and responding to the words so the child begins to learn the difference. (The EI professional recognizes the importance of maintaining a positive perception of the child and building responsive interactions into the strategies used and applies her expert power to share unbiased information and create interventions that might be effective).

Does not illustrate: The EI professional identifies that using such similar words would be too difficult for the child at this point and tells the family to keep a list of words they want the child to learn and, when it's time, they can begin to integrate them into routine activities.

Appendix A

5. Openly and Honestly Collaborate and Communicate, and Demonstrate Confidence

Prior to the family's appointment with a developmental pediatrician, the EI professional suspects that the doctor might raise the possibility of an autism spectrum disorder (ASD) diagnosis.

Illustrates: The EI professional brings up that, while he is unsure what diagnosis—if any—might be discussed, the doctor could identify the possibility of ASD. The EI professional shares any related observations and asks the family about their thoughts, feelings, and questions about the potential diagnosis. Together, the FPP lists objective data and questions to share with the doctor.

Does not illustrate: The EI professional does not say anything to the family since (1) the doctor may not bring it up, and (2) it is the doctor's responsibility to diagnose. After the doctor's appointment, the family expresses shock when the doctor suggested the possibility of ASD. The family asks the professional whether he ever suspected that might happen.

6. View Each Partnership Member as an Equal Member of the Team

The FPP completes an assessment, gathering information from all team members to synthesize into a functional, cross-domain report.

Illustrates: The results and impressions across all team members (including the family) are merged, resulting in one cohesive report that represents the perspectives of all team members.

Does not illustrate: The results and impressions across professional team members are merged. Results gleaned from the family are listed as "reported" and the family's perspectives are identified as either in agreement with or divergent from the professionals' perspectives.

7. Dig Deeper to Truly Understand

The EI professional splits her visits between times when the parents are home with the child and when the grandmother is caring for the child. The EI professional observed that the grandmother completes many tasks for the child, such as dressing the child and feeding the child.

Illustrates: The EI professional notes the strategy of "adult help" and asks the grandmother why she chooses to help him with these tasks. The grandmother shares that she wants to get the child ready to learn and doesn't want intervention time usually spent in play activities "wasted" with these tasks. The EI professional identifies the learning opportunities available during these routine activities and suggests that they can come up with strategies to help the child learn during those times, in addition to during play.

Does not illustrate: The EI professional assumes it is part of the grandmother's culture to do everything for the child. Since the EI professional wants to be culturally responsive, he chooses not to discuss this with the family. However, he continues to be concerned as the strategies he developed with the child's parents are not being utilized consistently across caregivers.

APPENDIX B

Family-Professional Partnership Practices

1. **Differentiate ways of knowing and professional decisions**
    1.1. Know and apply the developmental research on cultural differences in parenting
        1.1.1. Reflect on whether any differences in approaches between the EI professional and family are due to focusing on different outcomes
        1.1.2. Reflect on the EI professional's beliefs in how children learn as well as the professional's larger priorities of what children should learn and then, for each family, determine whether any differences in approaches are due to these different beliefs and priorities even when focused on the same outcomes
    1.2. Know and apply the developmental research on universal approaches
        1.2.1. Reflect on universal approaches to promote child learning and development; identify what those universals look like through the professional's own individual cultural lens and then, for each family, determine whether differences in approaches are alternate ways of meeting the same universals (strategies or outcomes)
    1.3. Utilize available resources to reflect on the professional's own cultural lens and how it might impact the professional's interactions with families
        1.3.1. Reflect on the professional's interactions with each family to identify ways they applied and could further enhance culturally responsive practices
    1.4. Know and apply the evidence base for meeting specific child outcomes
        1.4.1. Draw from what is currently known about a particular practice, which may not yet be deemed "evidence-based," and decide which practices to share with families and other team members

1.4.2. Use data-based decision making to determine child progress and how well the family implements the evidence-based practices (i.e., fidelity) to decide whether to continue or change the intervention
1.5. Know and apply evidence-based practices for supporting family use of evidence-based practices
1.5.1. Draw from and apply with fidelity evidence-based practices that effectively support families as they obtain new ways to promote their child's learning and development
1.6. Utilize available resources to develop an evidence-based practice toolbox
1.6.1. Seek out resources that enhance the professional's effective use of a variety of evidence-based practices that are shared with the FPP to inform EI decisions
1.7. Identify and manage professional's own emotional needs to focus on meeting early intervention's vision
1.8. Share the evidence base freely and plainly
1.8.1. Collaborate with the family to weigh the pros and cons of different potential decisions to meet desired family priorities and expected outcomes
1.9. Continually verify that interventions are meeting the family's priorities
1.10. Fill the EI professional toolbox with a variety of evidence-based practices

2. Appreciate family priorities, values, and culture

2.1. Intervene within the family's routine activities, attuned to the family's individual culture
2.2. Support the family in parenting the way they want to parent
2.3. Develop comfort and competence in purposely seeking to understand each family's partnership style, interacting and working accordingly, and eliciting feedback to assure the professional's interactions are indeed responsive to that partnership style
2.4. Effectively apply the active ingredients for coaching families, blended into the family's style of parenting and partnering
2.5. Encourage the family to share their thoughts and ideas first before giving the professional's perspective
2.6. Use "constant communication" to assess and revisit any decisions made
2.7. Apply responsive partnering regardless of role

3. Build family engagement

3.1. Identify the current engagement level of each family and intentionally use specific strategies that encourage families to engage at increasingly more active levels
3.2. Express an attitude of caring
    3.2.1. Incorporate care into their work by collaborating as thinking and feeling individuals
    3.2.2. Recognize care as a professionally valuable attitude, and seek out supports, if needed, to feel confident and competent in conveying a caring attitude
3.3. Set shared expectations
    3.3.1. Explore with families how early intervention works, ensure that families understand and appreciate these expectations, and then revisit these concepts as needed should family engagement wane
    3.3.2. Situate early intervention within the families' perceptions of parenting, child development, and disability rather than trying to convince families to change their beliefs to fit early intervention
3.4. Assure family relevance
    3.4.1. Explicitly attend to what families came to early intervention for—the family's priorities and outcomes, during the particular times the family is looking for EI support (i.e., family-identified routine activities)—and assure progress toward meeting those priorities and outcomes is seen by both FPP members
    3.4.2. Assure that supports are relevant and timely by asking families to identify the focus (i.e., priorities) for that particular visit
    3.4.3. Observe child behaviors and wonder with families to commingle professional-identified developmental expectations with family expectations to create meaningful interventions in which families want to engage
    3.4.4. Discuss with the family the active ingredients of potential interventions and together identify ways to modify or substitute interventions to better fit the family's culture, without reducing its effectiveness
3.5. Expect family engagement
    3.5.1. Value family choice around EI outcomes, approaches, and strategies, and provide interventions according to the choices each family makes
    3.5.2. Ask families how they wish to communicate between visits and use those modes to nurture engagement

3.6. Listen with heart and mind
3.7. Prioritize the family's questions
3.8. Trust in the partnership and all partnership members

4. Recognize the power of partnership members

4.1. Frame early intervention as a developmental promotion program
4.2. Use words and actions that reflect the developmental promotion frame
4.3. Use assessment instruments that allow for flexible administration to demonstrate the extent of child abilities while minimizing items inappropriate for the child to attempt
4.4. Use open-ended assessment instruments and less-structured procedures to gather assessment data from families
4.5. Blend strategies that both enhance quality parent–child interaction and child developmental outcomes within the multiple opportunities afforded in everyday family life
4.6. Analyze the goodness of fit of the family's responsive caregiving approaches to the child's interaction style and, if needed, partner with the family to enhance those approaches to foster powerful relationships
4.7. Identify and facilitate the achievement of family outcomes as a means to family quality of life
4.8. Recognize and respond to the needs of families of children with developmental delays or disabilities
4.9. Promote family self-efficacy versus dependence
4.10. Utilize expert power in a manner that is individualized according to child strengths and needs, family priorities, and the characteristics of everyday family life
4.11. Recognize that institutions hold power and EI professionals represent those institutions
4.12. Employ professional power to navigate the early intervention system
4.13. Explicitly discuss and act on the family's strengths and power
4.14. Provide unbiased information for the family so they can make informed decisions
4.15. Recognize and remedy when role and expertise power conflict
4.16. Articulate and act in accordance with the family's power
4.17. Use the power of the professional
4.18. Recognize and respond to signs that the family does not feel powerful in the family–professional partnership
4.19. Take the lead in ensuring the family takes the lead
4.20. Encourage all partners to weigh in on decisions to achieve a "balanced relationship"

Appendix B

4.21. Be as equally open and honest about professional's own strengths and needs as asked of the family
4.22. Acknowledge and appreciate when families take the power they deserve and share the power they have
4.23. Focus on the ultimate goal of family empowerment

5. Openly and honestly collaborate and communicate, and demonstrate confidence

5.1. Be positive, respectful, and sensitive to the family's individual culture
5.2. Allow families to communicate honestly so that they may agree and disagree with the professional
5.3. Talk about misunderstandings openly and calmly to better comprehend the family's perspective
5.4. Make sure each family feels more empowered and skilled (i.e., confident and competent) to support their child's development
5.5. Assess the context of priorities with families and brainstorm recommendations that can be integrated in family-established routines
5.6. Build multiple trustworthy relationships
    5.6.1. Strive to ensure each family member is at ease and trusts the professional
5.7. Tell families it's not personal (for the professional)
    5.7.1. Take comments from families objectively and respond supportively
5.8. Spend most of the visit time talking to the family to meet child, family, and parenting outcomes
    5.8.1. Spend almost all intervention time interacting with those family members who will be implementing the strategies between visits
5.9. Check in with the family on goodness of fit
    5.9.1. Use asking as a key to finding a better fit for the family in the intervention process

6. View each partnership member as an equal member of the team

6.1. Recognize what professional team members are learning from each family just like the reciprocal learning that occurs from other disciplinary professionals in transdisciplinary teaming
6.2. See each family–professional partnership as a separate team and take the time to develop that team
6.3. View families as competent in their role, while supporting them in learning new competencies
6.4. Value and utilize family perceptions and ideas

6.5. Invite all eligible families to apply for opportunities to contribute to the field, such as serving on an EI committee or participating in a research project
    6.5.1. Share opportunities so individual families can decide for themselves whether they want to participate
6.6. Ensure the family is involved whenever the early intervention team meets to come to consensus or make decisions, conveying that the family is truly appreciated for their disciplinary expertise
6.7. Recognize that families are distinct from professionals—in their contributions to, investment in, and impact on the team and achieving team outcomes
6.8. Adopt a "figuring it out together" perspective
6.9. Scaffold families to achieve their teaming roles
    6.9.1. Support families in identifying specific outcomes and contribute professional expertise to determining developmental steps and intervention strategies to scaffold families in the consensus decision-making process
6.10. Identify, relate, and apply the family's perception of a team and teaming
    6.10.1. Appreciate the influence of the family's perspectives and previous experiences on their readiness to team, and guide the family as they build teaming skills within their comfort zone
    6.10.2. Recognize that families will differ in how they view professional team members and are flexible and fluid in how each team interacts according to the parameters set by the individual family
6.11. Assume positive intent, with or without the "why"
    6.11.1. Create a safe space and initiate a discussion with the family to understand the reasons for their actions, replacing the hypothesized "why" with the actual reason
    6.11.2. Recognize that the reason the professional assigned to a family's actions is not necessarily accurate, and reframe any deficit-based assumptions into strengths, whether or not that strength is known
6.12. Question denial
    6.12.1. Avoid attributing families' behaviors as denial and seek to understand each family's perspectives

7. Dig deeper to truly understand

7.1. Explicitly mine the learning strategies occurring within routine activities and the family's perceptions behind those strategies to understand the strengths the family brings to early intervention

Appendix B

7.2. Uncover family strengths in helping their child learn
    7.2.1. Become a "fly on the wall" to see what families do to promote their child's learning and development in everyday life
    7.2.2. Combine observations and discussions to truly understand the breadth of learning strategies used and why they are used so the family–professional partnership can then plan strengths-based interventions
7.3. Plan interventions based on family strengths
    7.3.1. Design and implement interventions that are fully aligned to the family, including their parenting style, how they think about their child's learning and development, and what kind of help they want from early intervention
7.4. Understand first, then plan interventions
7.5. See through the eyes of the family
7.6. Use the process to build a mutually trusting relationship
    7.6.1. Trust families can think about and utilize learning strategies that promote child development because families already are thinking about and using strategies
7.7. Provide the "just right" support
7.8. Watch out for the early childhood challenge

8. Use practices that span all seven partnership concepts

8.1. Explore the professional's understanding of culture and how cultural differences can influence family and professional behaviors and, therefore, the family–professional partnership
8.2. Identify the values, beliefs, and attitudes inherent in the partnership concepts and lessons learned; explore the alignment to their own values, beliefs, and attitudes; and seek resources to reframe any misalignment
8.3. Continually seek feedback to understand and respond to changes in families' expectations for, and interactions within, the family–professional partnership
8.4. Recognize and respect the vulnerability and trust that families have invested in the family–professional partnership
8.5. Actively build partnerships with families to jointly carry out the data-based process of questioning, strategizing, and analyzing
8.6. Avoid assumptions by explicitly asking families for their thoughts, opinions, perceptions, and reasoning, and then accept the family's response as truthful
8.7. Recognize and embrace the uniqueness of each family–professional partnership; what "worked" for one family may or may not work for another

8.8. Appreciate and facilitate, rather than become discouraged, when a change in partnership members is needed
8.9. Reflect on how the partnership concepts work best within each individual family–professional partnership
8.10. Reflect on and then respond to what the family–professional partnership concepts look like in each early intervention process and with each family

APPENDIX C

Guiding Questions for Exploring Family and Professional Reflections

Readers can reflect on the following questions as they analyze the family and professional reflections in each chapter:

1. How were the family and professional reflections the same? How were they different from each other? In what ways do those differences matter to developing and sustaining a successful family–professional partnership? In what ways are those differences irrelevant to the FPP process?
2. What practices or interactions described in the reflections feel comfortable to you and why? Which ones are uncomfortable and why?
3. How do you think the family and professional's beliefs and attitudes contributed to the success of the partnership?
4. What "aha!" moments resulted from these reflections? What could you do, or do you do, to implement those "aha!" moments with each family you support?
5. How do you think the family–professional partnership continued to evolve after the time described in the reflection?

References

Abry, T., Hulleman, C., & Rimm-Kaufman, S. (2015). Using indices of fidelity to intervention core components to identify program active ingredients. *American Journal of Evaluation, 36*(3), 320–338. doi:10.1177/1098214014557009

Aldridge, J., Kilgo, J. L., & Bruton, A. K. (2015). Transforming transdisciplinary early intervention and early childhood special education through intercultural education. *International Journal of Early Childhood Special Education, 7*(2), 343–360.

Aldridge, J., Kilgo, J. L., & Christensen, L. M. (2014). Turning culture upside down: The role of transcultural education. *Social Studies Research and Practice, 9*(2), 107–119.

Al Khateeb, J. M., Al Hadidi, M. S., & Al Khatib, A. J. (2015). Addressing the unique needs of Arab American children with disabilities. *Journal of Child and Family Studies, 24,* 2432–2440. doi:10.1007/s10826-014-0046-x

Amatea, E., Cholewa, B., & Mixon, K. (2012). Low-income and/or ethnic minority families influencing preservice teachers' attitudes about working with low-income and/or ethnic minority families. *Urban Education, 47,* 801–834.

Aubin, T., & Mortenson, P. (2015). Experiences of early transdisciplinary teams in pediatric community rehabilitation. *Infants & Young Children, 28*(2), 165–181. doi:10.1097/IYC.0000000000000033

Bailey, D., Raspa, M., & Fox, L. (2012). What is the future of family outcomes and family-centered services? *Topics in Early Childhood Special Education, 31*(4), 216–223. doi:10.1177/027112141142077

Barrera, I., Kramer, L., & Macpherson, T. D. (2012). *Skilled dialogue: Strategies for responding to cultural diversity in early childhood.* Baltimore, MD: Brookes.

Beneke, M., & Cheatham, G. (2016). Inclusive, democratic family–professional partnerships: (Re)conceptualizing culture and language in teacher preparation. *Topics in Early Childhood Special Education, 35*(4), 234–244. doi:10.1177/0271121415581611

Bernheimer, L. P., & Keogh, B. K. (1995). Weaving interventions into the fabric of everyday life: An approach to family assessment. *Topics in Early Childhood Special Education, 15,* 415–433. doi:10.1177/027112149501500402

Bernheimer, L. P., & Weisner, T. (2007). "Let me just tell you what I do all day . . . " The family story at the center of intervention research and practice. *Infants & Young Children, 20*(3), 192–201.

Blue-Banning, M., Summers, J. A., Frankland, H. C., Nelson, L. L., & Beegle, G. (2004). Dimensions of family and professional partnerships: Constructive guidelines for collaboration. *Exceptional Children, 70*(2), 167–184.

Bornstein, M. (2002). Parenting infants. In M. Bornstein (Ed.), *Handbook of parenting: Vol. 1. Children and parenting* (pp. 3–44). Mahwah, NJ: Erlbaum.

Bronfenbrenner, U. (1979). *The ecology of human development: Experiments by nature and design.* Cambridge, MA: Harvard University Press.

Bronfenbrenner, U. (1993). The ecology of cognitive development: Research models and fugitive findings. In R. H. Wozniak & K. W. Fischer (Eds.), *Development in context: Acting and thinking in specific environments* (pp. 3–44). Hillsdale, NJ: Erlbaum.

Bronfenbrenner, U. (1999). Environments in developmental perspective: Theoretical and operational models. In S. L. Friedman & T. D. Wachs (Eds.), *Measuring environment across the life span: Emerging methods and concepts* (pp. 3–28). Washington, DC: American Psychological Association.

Bronfenbrenner, U. (2002). Preparing a world for the infant in the twenty-first century: The research challenge. In J. Gomes-Pedro, J. K. Nugent, J. G. Young, & T. B. Brazelton (Eds.), *The infant and family in the twenty-first century* (pp. 45–52). New York, NY: Brunner-Routledge.

Bronson, K. (2005). The culture of an early intervention home visit. *Journal of Early Childhood Research, 3*, 51–76. doi:10.1177/1476718X05051346

Brotherson, M. J., Summers, J. A., Naig, L., Kyzar, K., Friend, A., Epley, P., . . . Turnbull, A. (2010). Partnership patterns: Addressing emotional needs in early intervention. *Topics in Early Childhood Special Education, 30*, 32–45. doi:10.1177/0271121409360068

Brown, J., & Woods, J. (2016). Parent-implemented communication intervention: Sequential analysis of triadic relationships. *Topics in Early Childhood Special Education, 36*(2), 115–124. doi:10.1177/0271121416628200

Bruder, M. (2010). Coordinating services with families. In R. A. McWilliam (Ed.), *Working with young children with special needs* (pp. 93–126). New York, NY: Guilford Press.

Bryan, M. (2014). The significance of empowerment in the field of health and human services. *Journal of Human Services, 34*(1), 111–116.

Busch-Rossnagel, N. (2005). First, do no harm: Culturally centered measurement for early intervention. In J. Tremble & C. Fisher (Eds.), *The handbook of ethical research with ethnocultural populations and communities* (pp. 51–64). Thousand Oaks, CA: Sage.

Campbell, P. H., & Sawyer, L. B. (2007). Supporting learning opportunities in natural settings through participation-based services. *Journal of Early Intervention, 29*, 287–305. doi:10.1177/105381510702900402

Carlson, V., & Harwood, R. (1999/2000). Understanding and negotiating cultural differences concerning early developmental competence: The six raisin solution. *Zero to Three, 20*(3), 19–24.

Carroll, D. W. (2013). Stress, coping, and growth. In D. W. Carroll (Ed.), *Families of children with developmental disabilities: Understanding stress and opportunities for growth* (pp. 31–44). Washington, DC: American Psychological Association.

Cheatham, G., & Santos, R. (2009). Why won't they just cooperate? Understanding how cultural values impact how we team with families. In C. Peterson, L. Fox, & A. Santos (Eds.), *Quality inclusive services in a diverse society* (Young

Exceptional Children Monograph Series No. 11). Missoula, MT: Division for Early Childhood (of the Council for Exceptional Children).

Chiarello, L., Palisano, R., Bartlett, D. J., & Westcott, S. (2011). A multivariate model of determinants of change in gross motor abilities and engagement in self-care and play of young children with cerebral palsy. *Physical & Occupational Therapy in Pediatrics, 31*(2), 150–168. doi: 10.3109/01942638.2010.525601

Clarà, M. (2014). What is reflection? Looking for clarity in an ambiguous notion. *Journal of Teacher Education.* Advance online publication. doi:0.1177/0022487114552028

Coogle, C. G., Guerette, A. R., & Hanline, M. F. (2013). Early intervention experiences of families of children with an autism spectrum disorder: A qualitative pilot study. *Early Childhood Research and Practice, 15*(1), 1–11.

Cook, B. G., & Cook, S. C. (2011). Unraveling evidence-based practices in special education. *The Journal of Special Education, 47*(2), 71–82. doi: 10.1177/0022466911420877

Cook, B. G., & Odom, S. L. (2013). Evidence-based practices and implementation science in special education. *Exceptional Children, 79*(2), 135–144.

Deci, E., & Ryan, R. (2000). The "what" and "why" of goal pursuits: Human needs and the self-determination of behavior. *Psychological Inquiry, 11*(4), 227–268.

Diamond, K., & Kontos, S. (2004). Families' resources and accommodations: Toddlers with Down syndrome, cerebral palsy, and developmental delay. *Journal of Early Intervention, 26*, 253–265. doi:10.1177/105381510402600402

Di Santo, A., Timmons, K., & Pelletier, J. (2016). "Mommy that's the exit.": Empowering homeless mothers to support their children's daily literacy experiences. *Journal of Early Childhood Literacy, 16*, 145–170. doi:10.1177/1468798415577872

Division for Early Childhood (DEC). (2010). *Position statement: Responsiveness to ALL children, families, and professionals: Integrating cultural and linguistic diversity into policy and practice.* Retrieved from Division for Early Childhood website under "Family Culture, Values, and Language": www.dec-sped.org/#!position-statements/oqa2f

Division for Early Childhood (DEC). (2014). *Recommended practices in early intervention/early childhood special education.* Retrieved from www.dec-sped.org/recommendedpractices

Dodici, B., Draper, D., & Peterson, C. (2003). Early parent–child interactions and early literacy development. *Topics in Early Childhood Special Education, 23*, 124–135. doi:10.1177/02711214030230030301

Doran, P., Mazur, A., & Llagas, C. (2012). Factors influencing culturally and linguistically diverse student and family needs. In R. Santos, G. Cheatham, & L. Duran (Eds.), *Supporting young children who are dual language learners with or at-risk for disabilities* (Young Exceptional Children Monograph Series No. 14). Missoula, MT: Division for Early Childhood (of the Council for Exceptional Children).

Dunst, C. J. (2000). Revisiting "Rethinking early intervention." *Topics in Early Childhood Special Education, 20*, 95–104.

Dunst, C. J. (2012). Parapatric speciation in the evolution of early intervention for infants and toddlers with disabilities and their families. *Topics in Early Childhood Special Education, 31*, 208–215. doi:10.1177/0271121411426904

Dunst, C. J., & Espe-Sherwindt, M. (2016). Family-centered practices in early childhood intervention. In B. Reichow, B. Boyd, E. Barton, & S. Odom (Eds.), *Handbook of early childhood special education* (pp. 37–55). [Cham,] Switzerland: Springer International.

Dunst, C. J., Raab, M., Trivette, C. M., & Swanson, J. (2010). Community-based everyday child learning opportunities. In R. A. McWilliam (Ed.), *Working with young children with special needs* (pp. 60–92). New York, NY: Guilford Press.

Dunst, C. J., & Trivette, C. M. (1996). Empowerment, effective helpgiving practices and family-centered care. *Pediatric Nursing, 22*(4). Retrieved from go.galegroup.com/ps/i.do?p=AONE&sw=w&u=cuny_gradctr&v=2.1&id=GALE%7CA19138566&it=r&asid=f8cfba42ae06bc4bb96a0a292acf585a

Dunst, C. J., & Trivette, C. M. (2009a). Capacity-building family systems intervention practices. *Journal of Family Social Work, 12,* 119–143. dx.doi.org/10.1080/10522150802713322

Dunst, C. J., & Trivette, C. M. (2009b). Let's be PALS: An evidence-based approach to professional development. *Infants & Young Children, 22,* 164–176. doi:10.1097/IYC.0b013e3181abe169

Dunst, C. J., & Trivette, C. M. (2009c). Using research evidence to inform and evaluate early childhood intervention practices. *Topics in Early Childhood Special Education, 29,* 40–53. doi:10.1177/0271121408329227

Dunst, C. J., Trivette, C. M., Davis, M., & Cornwell, J. (1988). Enabling and empowering families of children with health impairments. *Children's Health Care, 17*(2), 71–81.

Dunst, C. J., Trivette, C. M., & Hamby, D. (2007). Meta-analysis of family-centered helpgiving practices research. *Mental Retardation and Developmental Disabilities Research Reviews, 13,* 370–378. doi:10.1002/mrdd.20176

Dunst, C. J., Trivette, C. M., & Hamby, D. (2010). A meta-analysis of the effectiveness of four adult learning methods and strategies. *International Journal of Continuing Education and Lifelong Learning, 3,* 91–112.

Dunst, C. J., Trivette, C. M., & Raab, M. (2013). An implementation science framework for conceptualizing and operationalizing fidelity in early childhood intervention studies. *Journal of Early Intervention, 35,* 85–101. doi:10.1177/1053815113502235

Dworkin, P. (2000). Preventive health care and anticipatory guidance. In J. P. Shonkoff & S. J. Meisels (Eds.), *Handbook of early childhood intervention* (2nd ed., pp. 327–338). Cambridge, England: Cambridge University Press.

Early Intervention Program for Infants and Toddlers with Disabilities Rule of 2011, 34 C.F.R. §303 (2011)

Edwards, P. A. (2016). *New ways to engage parents: Strategies and tools for teachers and leaders, K–12.* New York, NY: Teachers College Press.

Engster, D. (2005). Rethinking care theory: The practice of caring and the obligation to care. *Hypatia, 20*(3), 50–74.

Epley, P., Summers, J., & Turnbull, A. (2011). Family outcomes of early intervention: Families' perceptions of need, services, and outcomes. *Journal of Early Intervention, 33*(3), 201–219. doi:10.1177/1053815111425929

Etscheidt, S., Curran, C., & Sawyer, C. (2012). Promoting reflection in teacher preparation programs: A multilevel model. *Teacher Education and Special Education, 35*(1), 7–26.

References

Evans, D. L., Feit, M. D., & Trent, T. (2015). African American parents and attitudes about child disability and early intervention services. *Journal of Social Service Research, 42*(1), 96–112. http://dx.doi.org/10.1080/01488376.2015.1081118

Fialka, J. (2001). The dance of partnership: Why do my feet hurt? Strengthening the parent–professional partnership. *Young Exceptional Children, 4*(2), 21–27. Retrieved from www.danceofpartnership.com/DanceArticleSept06.pdf

Fingerhut, P. E., Piro, J., Sutton, A., Campbell, R., Lewis, C., Lawji, D., & Martinez, N. (2013). Family-centered principles implemented in home-based, clinic-based, and school-based pediatric settings. *The American Journal of Occupational Therapy, 67*, 228–235. dx.doi.org/10.5014/ajot.2013.006957

Fleming, J., Sawyer, B., & Campbell, P. H.(2011). Early intervention providers' perspectives about implementing participation-based practices. *Topics in Early Childhood Special Education, 30*, 233–244. doi:10.1177/0271121410371986

Fraiberg, L. (Ed.). (1987). *Selected writings of Selma Fraiberg*. Columbus: Ohio State University Press.

Friesen, A., Hanson, M., & Martin, K. (2015). In the eyes of the beholder: Cultural considerations in interpreting children's behaviors. *Young Exceptional Children, 18*(4), 19–30. doi:10.1177/1096250614535222

Gallagher, P., Fialka, J., Rhodes, C., & Arceneaux, C. (2002). Working with families: Rethinking denial. *Young Exceptional Children, 5*(2), 11–17.

Gallimore, R., Weisner, T. S., Bernheimer, L. P., Guthrie, D., & Nihira, K. (1993). Family responses to young children with developmental delays: Accommodation activity in ecological and cultural context. *American Journal of Mental Retardation, 98*, 185–206.

Gallimore, R., Weisner, T. S., Kaufman, S., & Bernheimer, L. P. (1989). The social construction of ecocultural niches: Family accommodation of developmentally delayed children. *American Journal of Mental Retardation, 98*(2), 185–206.

Gauvain, M. (2013). Sociocultural contexts of development. In P. D. Zelazo (Ed.), *The Oxford handbook of developmental psychology, Vol. 2: Self and other*. New York, NY: Oxford University Press. doi:10.1093/oxfordhb/9780199958474.013.0017

Geller, E. (2015, December). *Integrating reflective practice into one allied discipline*. Session presented at Supporting and Retaining Early Intervention Families Through Reflective Practice workshop at the New York City Bureau of Early Intervention, Department of Health and Mental Hygiene, New York, NY.

Geller, E., & Foley, G. (2009). Expanding the "ports of entry" for speech–language pathologists: A relational and reflective model for clinical practice. *American Journal of Speech–language Pathology, 18*(1), 4–21.

Gilkerson, L., & Shahmoon-Shanok, R. (2000). Relationships for growth: Cultivating reflective practice in infant, toddler, and preschool programs. In J. D. Osofsky & H. E. Fitzgerald (Eds.), *WAIMH handbook of infant mental health: Vol. 2. Early intervention, evaluation, and assessment* (pp. 3–32). New York, NY: John Wiley.

González, N., Moll, L., & Amanti, C. (2005). *Funds of knowledge: Theorizing practices in households, communities, and classrooms*. Mahwah, NJ: Lawrence Erlbaum.

Guralnick, M. J. (1997). Second generation research in the field of early intervention. In M. J. Guralnick (Ed.), *The effectiveness of early intervention* (pp. 3–20). Baltimore, MD: Brookes.

Guralnick, M. J. (2011). Why early intervention works: A systems perspective. *Infants & Young Children, 24*, 6–28. doi:10.1097/IYC.0b013e3182002cfe

Halle, T., Metz, A., & Martinez-Beck, I. (2013). *Applying implementation science in early childhood programs and systems.* Baltimore, MD: Brookes.

Hanson, M., & Espinosa, L. (2016). Culture, ethnicity, and linguistic diversity: Implications for early childhood special education. In B. Reichow, B. Boyd, E. Barton, & S. Odom (Eds.), *Handbook of early childhood special education* (pp. 455–471). [Cham,] Switzerland: Springer International.

Hanson, M., & Lynch, E. (2010). Working with families from diverse backgrounds. In R. A. McWilliam (Ed.), *Working with young children with special needs* (pp. 147–174). New York, NY: Guilford Press.

Hansuvadha, N. (2009). Compromise in collaborating with families: Perspectives of beginning special education teachers. *Journal of Early Childhood Teacher Education, 30*(4), 346–362. doi:10.1080/10901020903320270

Harbin, G. L., McWilliam, R. A., & Gallagher, J. J. (2000). Services for young children with disabilities and their families. In J. P. Shonkoff & S. J. Meisels (Eds.), *Handbook of early childhood intervention* (2nd ed., pp. 387–415). Cambridge, England: Cambridge University Press.

Harn, B., Parisi, D., & Stoolmiller, M. (2013). Balancing fidelity with flexibility and fit: What do we really know about fidelity of implementation in schools? *Exceptional Children, 79*(2), 181–193.

Hebbeler, C., & Gerlach-Downie, S. (2002). Inside the black box of home visiting: A qualitative analysis of why intended outcomes were not achieved. *Early Childhood Research Quarterly, 17*, 28–51. doi:10.1016/S0885-2006(02)00128-X

Heffron, M., Ivins, B., & Weston, D. (2005). Finding an authentic voice: Use of self: Essential learning processes for relationship-based work. *Infants & Young Children, 18*(4), 323–336.

Individuals with Disabilities Education Act of 2004, 20 U.S.C. § 1400. (2004).

Innocenti, M. S., Roggman, L. A., & Cook, G. A. (2013). Using the PICCOLO with parents of children with a disability. *Infant Mental Health, 34*, 307–318. doi:10.1002/imhj.21394

Institute of Medicine. (2000). *From neurons to neighborhoods: The science of early childhood development.* Washington, DC: National Academies Press.

James, C., & Chard, G. (2010). A qualitative study of parental experiences of participation and partnership in an early intervention service. *Infants & Young Children, 23*, 275–285. doi:10.1097/IYC.0b013e3181f2264f

Jayaraman, G., Marvin, C., Knoche, L., & Bainter, S. (2015). Coaching conversations in early childhood programs: The contributions of coach and coachee. *Infants & Young Children, 28*(4), 323–336. doi:10.1097/IYC.0000000000000048

Jones-Harden, B., Denmark, N., & Saul, D. (2010). Understanding the needs of staff in Head Start programs: The characteristics, perceptions, and experiences of home visitors. *Children and Youth Services Review, 32*, 371–379.

Jung, L. A. (2010). Identifying families' supports and other resources. In R. A. McWilliam (Ed.), *Working with young children with special needs* (pp. 9–26). New York, NY: Guilford Press.

Jung, L. A., & McWilliam, R. A. (2005). Reliability and validity of scores on the IFSP rating scale. *Journal of Early Intervention, 27*, 125–136.

References

Kalyanpur, M., & Harry, B. (2012). *Cultural reciprocity in special education*. Baltimore, MD: Brookes.

Karst, J., & Van Hecke, A. (2012). Parent and family impact of autism spectrum disorders: A review and proposed model for intervention evaluation. *Clinical Child and Family Psychology Review, 15*, 247–277. doi:10.1007/s10567-012-0119-6

Keilty, B. (2008). Early intervention home visiting principles in practice: A reflective approach. *Young Exceptional Children, 11*(2), 29–40. doi:10.1177/1096250607311933

Keilty, B. (2013). Voices from the field: Developing and promoting early intervention expertise. *Young Exceptional Children, 26*(3), 36–38. doi:10.1177/1096250607311933

Keilty, B. (2016). *The early intervention guidebook for families and professionals: Partnering for success* (2nd ed.). New York, NY: Teachers College Press.

Keilty, B., & Freund, M. (2005). Caregiver–child interaction in infants and toddlers born extremely premature. *Journal of Pediatric Nursing, 20*(3), 181–189.

Keilty, B., & Galvin, K. (2006). Physical and social adaptations families make to promote learning in everyday experiences. *Topics in Early Childhood Special Education, 26*(4), 219–233.

Keilty, B., & Galvin, K. (2014). *Family Strengths in Child Learning (FamSCL): Program planning for effective family–professional partnerships*. Unpublished protocol, Hunter College, City University of New York, New York.

Kellar-Guenther, Y., Rosenberg, S. A., Block, S. R., & Robinson, C. C. (2014). Parent involvement in early intervention: What role does setting play? *Early Years, 34*(1), 81–93. doi:10.1080/09575146.2013.823382

Kellegrew, D. (2000). Constructing daily routines: A qualitative examination of mothers with young children with disabilities. *The American Journal of Occupational Therapy, 54*(3), 252–259.

Keller, H., & Kärtner, J. (2013). Development: The cultural solution of universal developmental tasks. In M. Gelfand, C. Chi-yue, and Y.-Y. Hong (Eds.), *Advances in culture and psychology* (Vol. 3, pp. 63–116). New York, NY: Oxford University Press. doi:10.1093/acprof:oso/9780199930449.003.0002

Kemp, P., & Turnbull, A. (2014). Coaching with parents in early intervention: An interdisciplinary research synthesis. *Infants & Young Children, 27*, 305–324.

Ketelaar, M., Vermeer, A., Helders, P., & Hart, H. (1998). Parenting participation in intervention programs for children with cerebral palsy: A review of the research. *Topics in Early Childhood Special Education, 18*, 108–117.

Khetani, M., Cohn, E., Orsmond, G., Law, M., & Coster, W. (2013). Parent perspectives of participation in home and community activities when receiving Part C early intervention services. *Topics in Early Childhood Special Education, 32*, 234–245. doi:10.1177/0271121411418004

Kim, J. M., & Mahoney, G. (2004). The effects of mother's style of interaction on children's engagement: Implications for using responsive interventions with parents. *Topics in Early Childhood Special Education, 24*, 31–38.

Kingsley, K., & Mailloux, Z. (2013). Evidence of the effectiveness of different service delivery models in early intervention services. *The American Journal of Occupational Therapy, 67*(4), 431–436. Retrieved from dx.doi.org/10.5014/ajot.2013.006171

Kong, N., & Carta, J. (2013). Responsive interaction interventions for children with or at risk for developmental delays: A research synthesis. *Topics in Early Childhood Special Education, 33,* 4–17. doi:10.1177/0271121411426486

Krauss, M. W. (2000). Family assessment within early intervention programs. In J. P. Shonkoff & S. J. Meisels (Eds.), *Handbook of early childhood intervention* (2nd ed., pp. 290–308). Cambridge, England: Cambridge University Press.

Kresak, K., Gallagher, P., & Kelley, S. (2014). Grandmothers raising grandchildren with disabilities: Sources of support and family quality of life. *Journal of Early Intervention, 36,* 3–17. doi:10.1177/1053815114542506

LaForme Fiss, A., Chiarello, L. A., Bartlett, D. J., Palisano, R., Jeffries, L., Almasri, N., & Chang, H-J. (2013). Family ecology of young children with cerebral palsy. *Child: Care, Health and Development, 40,* 562–571. doi:10.1111/cch.12062

Lalvani, P. (2015). Disability, stigma and otherness: Perspectives of parents and teachers. *International Journal of Disability, Development and Education, 62,* 379–393. doi:10.1080/1034912X.2015.1029877

Ledford, J., & Wolery, M. (2013). Procedural fidelity: An analysis of measurement and reporting practices. *Journal of Early Intervention, 35,* 173–193. doi:10.1177/1053815113515908

Lee, Y. H. (2015). The paradox of early intervention: Families' participation driven by professionals throughout service process. *International Journal of Child Care, 9*(4). doi:10.1186/s40723-015-0007-x

Lieberman-Betz, R. (2015). A systematic review of fidelity of implementation in parent-mediated early communication intervention. *Topics in Early Childhood Special Education, 35,* 15–27. doi:10.1177/0271121414557282

Luo, R., & Tamis-LeMonda, C. (2016). Mothers' verbal and nonverbal strategies in relation to infants' object-directed actions in real time and across the first three years in ethnically diverse families. *Infancy, 21*(1), 65–89. doi:10.1111/infa.12099

Mahoney, G., Boyce, G., Fewell, R., Spiker, D., & Wheeden, C. (1998). The relationship of parent–child interaction to the effectiveness of early intervention services for at-risk children and children with disabilities. *Topics in Early Childhood Special Education, 18,* 5–17. doi:10.1177/027112149801800104

Mahoney, G., Robinson, C., & Perales, F. (2004). Early motor intervention: The need for new treatment paradigms. *Infants & Young Children, 17*(4), 291–300.

Mahoney, G., Spiker, D., & Boyce, G. (1996). Clinical assessments of parent–child interaction: Are professionals ready to implement this practice? *Topics in Early Childhood Special Education, 16*(1), 26–50.

Maul, C., & Singer, G. (2009). "Just good different things": Specific accommodations families make to positively adapt to their children with developmental disabilities. *Topics in Early Childhood Special Education, 29,* 155–170. doi:10.1177/0271121408328516

McCollum, J., & Yates, T. (1994). Dyad as focus, triad as means: A family-centered approach to supporting parent–child interactions. *Infants & Young Children, 6*(4), 54–63.

McConnell, S., & Rahn, N. (2016). Assessment in early childhood special education. In B. Reichow, B. Boyd, E. Barton, & S. Odom (Eds.), *Handbook of early childhood special education* (pp. 89–106). [Cham,] Switzerland: Springer International.

References

McWayne, C., Melzi, G., Schick, A., Kennedy, J., & Mundt, K. (2013). Defining family engagement among Latino Head Start parents: A mixed-methods measurement development study. *Early Childhood Research Quarterly, 28*(3), 593–607. dx.doi.org/10.1016/j.ecresq.2013.03.008

McWilliam, P. J. (2010). Talking to families. In R. A. McWilliam (Ed.), *Working with young children with special needs* (pp. 127–146). New York, NY: Guilford Press.

McWilliam, R. A. (2000). It's only natural . . . to have early intervention in the environments where it's needed. In S. Sandall & M. Ostrosky (Eds.), *Young exceptional children monograph series no. 2: Natural environments and inclusion* (pp. 17–26). Longmont, CO: Sopris West.

McWilliam, R. A. (2010a). Support-based home visiting. In R. A. McWilliam (Ed.), *Working with young children with special needs* (pp. 203–236). New York, NY: Guilford Press.

McWilliam, R. A. (2010b). Assessing families' needs with the Routines-Based Interview. In R. A. McWilliam (Ed.), *Working with young children with special needs* (pp. 27–59). New York, NY: Guilford Press.

McWilliam, R. A. (2012). Implementing and preparing for home visits. *Topics in Early Childhood Special Education, 31,* 224–231. doi:10.1177/0271121411426488

McWilliam, R. A. (2015). Future of early intervention with infants and toddlers for whom typical experiences are not effective. *Remedial and Special Education, 36*(1), 33–38. doi:10.1177/0741932514554105

McWilliam, R. A. (2016). Birth to three: Early intervention. In B. Reichow, B. Boyd, E. Barton, & S. Odom (Eds.), *Handbook of early childhood special education* (pp. 75–88). [Cham,] Switzerland: Springer International.

McWilliam, R. A., Casey, A., Ashley, D., Fielder, J., Rowley, P., DeJong, K., . . . Votava, K. (2011). Assessment of family-identified needs through the Routines-Based Interview. In M. McLean & P. Snyder (Eds.), *Gathering information to make informed decisions: Contemporary perspectives about assessment in early intervention and early childhood special education* (Young Exceptional Children Monograph Series No. 13, pp. 43–63). Missoula, MT: Division for Early Childhood (of the Council for Exceptional Children).

McWilliam, R. A., & Scott, S. (2001). A support approach to early intervention: A three-part framework. *Infants & Young Children, 13,* 55–66.

Minke, K., & Scott, M. (1995). Parent–professional relationships in early intervention: A qualitative investigation. *Topics in Early Childhood Special Education, 15*(3), 335–352.

Moll, L. (2015). Tapping into the "hidden" home and community resources of students. *Kappa Delta Pi Record, 51*(3), 114–117. doi:10.1080/00228958.2015.1056661

Moore, H., Barton, E., & Chironis, M. (2014). A program for improving toddler communication through parent coaching. *Topics in Early Childhood Special Education, 33,* 212–224. doi:10.1177/0271121413497520

Nagro, S., & Cornelius, K. (2013). Evaluating the evidence base of video analysis: A special education teacher development tool. *Teacher Education and Special Education, 36,* 312–329.

National Academies of Sciences, Engineering, and Medicine. (2016). *Parenting matters: Supporting parents of children ages 0–8.* Washington, DC: National Academies Press. doi:10.17226/21868

Neisworth, J., & Bagnato, S. (2004). The mismeasure of young children: The authentic assessment alternative. *Infants & Young Children, 17*(3), 198–212.

Ng, F., Tamis-LeMonda, C., Godfrey, E., Hunter, C., & Yoshikawa, H. (2012). Dynamics of mothers' goals for children in ethnically diverse populations across the first three years of life. *Social Development, 21*(4), 821–848. doi:10.1111/j.1467-9507.2012.00664.x

Noddings, N. (2013). *Caring: A feminine approach to ethics and moral education* (2nd ed.). Berkeley: University of California Press.

Odom, S. (2016). The role of theory in early childhood special education and early intervention. In B. Reichow, B. Boyd, E. Barton, & S. Odom (Eds.), *Handbook of early childhood special education* (pp. 21–36). [Cham,] Switzerland: Springer International.

Palisano, R. J., Chiarello, L. A., King, G. A., Novak, I., Stoner, T., & Fiss, A. (2012). Participation-based therapy for children with physical disabilities. *Disability & Rehabilitation, 34*(12), 1041–1052. doi:10.3109/09638288.2011.628740

Peterson, C., Luze, G., Eshbaugh, E., Jeon, H., & Ross Kantz, K. (2007). Enhancing parent–child interactions through home visiting: Promising practice or unfulfilled promise? *Journal of Early Intervention, 29*, 119–140. doi:10.1177/105381510702900205

Pierce, D. (2000). Maternal management of the home as a developmental play space for infants and toddlers. *The American Journal of Occupational Therapy, 54*(3), 290–299.

Pretti-Frontczak, K., Bagnato, S., Macy, M., & Sexton, D. (2011). Data-driven decision making to plan programs and promote performance. In C. Groak (Ed.), *Early childhood intervention: Shaping the future for children with special needs and their families* (pp. 55–80). Santa Barbara, CA: Praeger.

Raab, M., Dunst, C. J., Johnson, M., & Hamby, D. (2013). *Influences of a responsive interactional style on young children's language acquisition* (Everyday Child Language Learning Reports, No. 4). Asheville, NC: Puckett Institute.

Raikes, H., Roggman, L., Peterson, C., Brooks-Gunn, J., Chazan-Cohen, R., Zhang, X., & Schiffman, R. (2014). Theories of change and outcomes in home-based Early Head Start programs. *Early Childhood Research Quarterly, 29*, 574–585. Retrieved from dx.doi.org/10.1016/j.ecresq.2014.05.003

Raver, S. A., & Childress, D. C. (2014). Collaboration and teamwork with families and professionals. In S. A. Raver & D. C. Childress (Eds.), *Family-centered early intervention: Supporting infants and toddlers in natural environments* (pp. 31–52). Baltimore, MD: Brookes.

Reichow, B. (2016). Evidence-based practice in the context of early childhood special education. In B. Reichow, B. Boyd, E. Barton, & S. Odom (Eds.), *Handbook of early childhood special education* (pp. 107–121). [Cham,] Switzerland: Springer International.

Reichow, B., Boyd, B., Barton, E., & Odom, S. (Eds). (2016). *Handbook of early childhood special education*. [Cham,] Switzerland: Springer International.

Reyes, I., DaSilva Iddings, A., & Feller N. (2016). Building relationships with diverse students and families: A funds of knowledge perspective. *Journal of Early Childhood Literacy, 16*(1), 8–33. doi:10.1177/1468798415584692

References

Ridgley, R., Snyder, P., & McWilliam, R. A. (2014). Exploring type and amount of parent talk during individualized family service plan meetings. *Infants & Young Children, 27*(4), 345–358.

Roggman, L., Boyce, L., Cook, G., & Jump, V. (2001). Inside home visits: A collaborative look at process and quality. *Early Childhood Research Quarterly, 16*, 53–71. doi:10.1016/S0885-2006(01)00085-0

Rush, D., & Shelden, M. (2011). *The early intervention coaching handbook.* Baltimore, MD: Brookes.

Ryan, R., Deci, E., Fowler, R., Seligman, M., & Csikszentmihalyi, M. (2000). Self-determination theory and the facilitation of intrinsic motivation, social development, and well-being. *American Psychologist, 55*(1), 68–78.

Salisbury, C., Woods, J., & Copeland, C. (2010). Provider perspectives on adopting and using collaborative consultation in natural environments. *Topics in Early Childhood Special Education, 30*, 132–147.

Sameroff, A., & Fiese, B. (2000a). Models of development and developmental risk. In C. H. Zeanah (Ed.), *Handbook of infant mental health* (2nd ed., pp. 3–19). New York, NY: Guilford Press.

Sameroff, A., & Fiese, B. (2000b). Transactional regulation: The developmental ecology of early intervention. In J. P. Shonkoff & S. J. Meisels (Eds.), *Handbook of early childhood intervention* (2nd ed., pp. 135–159). Cambridge, England: Cambridge University Press.

Sandall, S., Schwartz, I., & Gauvreau, A. (2016). Using modifications and accommodations to enhance learning of young children with disabilities: Little changes that yield big impacts. In B. Reichow, B. Boyd, E. Barton, & S. Odom (Eds.), *Handbook of early childhood special education* (pp. 349–361). [Cham,] Switzerland: Springer International.

Santagata, R., & Angelici, G. (2010). Studying the impact of the lesson analysis framework on preservice teachers' abilities to reflect on videos of classroom teaching. *Journal of Teacher Education, 61*, 339–349.

Sass-Lehrer, M., Porter, A., & Wu, C. L. (2016). Families: Partnerships in practice. In M. Sass-Lehrer (Ed.), *Early intervention for deaf and hard-of-hearing infants, toddlers, and their families: Interdisciplinary perspectives* (pp. 65–103). New York, NY: Oxford University Press.

Schertz, H., Baker, C., Hurwitz, S., & Benner, L. (2011). Principles of early intervention reflected in toddler research in autism spectrum disorders. *Topics in Early Childhood Special Education, 31*, 4–21. doi:10.1177/0271121410382460

Sewell, T. (2012). Are we adequately preparing teachers to partner with families? *Early Childhood Education Journal, 40*, 259–263.

Shelden, M., & Rush, D. (2010). A primary-coach approach to teaming and supporting families in early childhood intervention. In R. A. McWilliam (Ed.), *Working with young children with special needs* (pp. 175–202). New York, NY: Guilford Press.

Shelden, M., & Rush, D. (2013). *The early intervention teaming handbook: The primary service provider approach.* Baltimore, MD: Brookes.

Shonkoff, J. P., & Hauser-Cram, P. (1987). Early intervention for disabled infants and their families: A quantitative analysis. *Pediatrics, 80*(5), 650–658.

Smaller, B. (1997, December 15). My baby is not on backwards—your baby is on backwards [cartoon]. *New Yorker.* Retrieved from www.condenaststore.com/-sp/My-baby-is-not-on-backwards-your-baby-is-on-backwards-New-Yorker-Cartoon-Prints_i8474320_.htm

Smith, G. J., Schmidt, M. M., Edelen-Smith, P. J., & Cook, B. G. (2013). Pasteur's Quadrant as the bridge linking rigor with relevance. *Exceptional Children, 79*(2) 147–161.

Smyth, C., Spicer, C., & Morgese, Z. (2014). Family voices at mealtime: Experiences with young children with visual impairment. *Topics in Early Childhood Special Education, 34,* 175–185. doi:10.1177/0271121414536622

Sokoly, M., & Dokecki, P. (1992). Ethical perspectives on family-centered early intervention. *Infants & Young Children, 4*(4), 23–32.

Spicer, P. (2010). Cultural influences on parenting. *Zero to Three, 30*(4), 28–32.

Spino, M., Dinnebeil, L., & McInerney, W. (2013). Social power and influence: Understanding its relevance in early childhood consultation. *Young Exceptional Children, 16*(4), 17–30. doi:10.1177/1096250613493191

Strozier, S. D., Flores, M. M., Hinton, V., Shippen, M., & Taylor, S. (2016). Interdisciplinary collaboration in teacher preparation to support students with exceptionalities. In F. E. Obiakor, A. Rieger, & A. F. Rotatori (Eds.), *Critical issues in preparing effective early childhood special education teachers for the 21st century classroom: Interdisciplinary perspectives* (pp. 59–69). Charlotte, NC: Information Age.

Sutherland, K., McLeod, B., Conroy, M., & Cox, J. (2013). Measuring implementation of evidence-based programs targeting young children at risk for emotional/behavioral disorders: Conceptual issues and recommendations. *Journal of Early Intervention, 35,* 129–149. doi:10.1177/1053815113515025

Taggart, G., & Wilson, A. (2005). *Promoting reflective thinking in teachers: 50 action strategies* (2nd ed.). Thousand Oaks, CA: Corwin Press.

Tamis-LeMonda, C., Song, L., Leavell, A., Kahana-Kalman, R., & Yoshikawa, H. (2012). Ethnic differences in mother–infant language and gestural communications are associated with specific skills in infants. *Developmental Science, 15*(3), 384–397. doi:10.1111/j.1467-7687.2012.01136.x

Test, D., Kemp-Inman, A., Diegelmann, K., Hitt, S., & Bethune, L. (2015). Are online sources for identifying evidence-based practices trustworthy? An evaluation. *Exceptional Children, 82,* 58–80. doi:10.1177/0014402915585477

Trivette, C. M., & Dunst, C. J. (1987). Proactive influences of social support in families of handicapped children. *Family Strengths, 8,* 391–405.

Trivette, C. M., Dunst, C. J., & Hamby, D. (2010). Influences of family-systems intervention practices on parent–child interaction and child development. *Topics in Early Childhood Special Education, 30,* 3–19. doi:10.1177/0271121410364250

Trivette, C. M., Dunst, C. J., Simkus, A., & Hamby, D. (2013). *Methods for increasing child participation in everyday learning opportunities* (Everyday Child Language Learning Reports, No. 7). Asheville, NC: Puckett Institute.

Turnbull, A., Blue-Banning, M., Turbiville, V., & Park, J. (1999). From parent education to partnership education: A call for a transformed focus. *Topics in Early Childhood Special Education, 19,* 164–172. doi:10.1177/027112149901900308

References

Turnbull, A., Turnbull, R., Erwin, E., Soodak, L., & Shogren, K. (2015). *Families, professionals, and exceptionality: Positive outcomes through partnerships and trust* (7th ed.). Upper Saddle River, NJ: Pearson Education.

Viola, J. J., Olson, B. D., Reed, S. F., Jimenez, T. R., & Smith, C. M. (2015). Building and strengthening collaborative community partnerships. In V. C. Scott & S. M. Wolfe (Eds.), *Community psychology: Foundations for practice* (pp. 237–261). Thousand Oaks, CA: Sage.

Wagner, M., Spiker, D., Linn, M. I., Gerlach-Downie, S., & Hernandez, F. (2003). Dimensions of parental engagement in home visiting programs: Exploratory study. *Topics in Early Childhood Special Education, 23*(4), 171–187.

Wainer, A., Hepburn, S., & Griffith, E. (2016). Remembering parents in parent–mediated early intervention: An approach to examining impact on parents and families. *Autism*. Advance online publication. doi:10.1177/1362361315622411

Williams, G., Rodin, G., Ryan, R., Grolnick, W., & Deci, E. (1998). Autonomous regulation and long-term medication adherence in adult outpatients. *Health Psychology, 17*(3), 269–276.

Yahya, R. (2015). Bridging home and school: Understanding immigrant mothers' cultural capital and concerns about play-based learning, *Early Years*. Advance online publication. doi:10.1080/09575146.2015.1110786

Ylitapio-Mäntylä, O. (2013). Reflecting caring and power in early childhood education: Recalling memories of educational practices. *Scandinavian Journal of Educational Research, 57*(3), 263–276. dx.doi.org/10.1080/00313831.2011.637230

Index

Abry, T., 16, 17
Accurate perceptions, 117
Achievement of family outcomes, 57
"Active ingredients," 16, 18, 35
Active participation, 39, 81
Adapting interventions, 15, 18
Advocacy, 2, 49, 50, 59, 66
Affective attunement, 43
Agenda setting, 62–63
Agreeing on strategies/goals, 29, 46, 64, 65, 72–73, 75–76, 86
Aldridge, J., 69–70, 71, 72, 73, 82, 83
Al Hadidi, M. S., 44, 70, 72
Al Khateeb, J. M., 29, 44, 70, 72
Al Khatib, A. J., 29, 44, 70, 72
Almasri, N., 100
Amanti, C., 99, 100
Amatea, E., 3
American Occupational Therapy Association, 16
American Physical Therapy Association, 16
American Speech-Language-Hearing Association, 16
Angelici, G., 8, 118
Applying supports, 39, 40
Approaches to parenting, 14–15
Arceneaux, C., 96, 97
Ashley, D., 5, 6, 96
Assessment, 36, 55, 72–73, 75, 77, 102, 103, 109
Assessment-to-intervention approach, 102
Assets focus, 54. *See also* Positive perception
Associative power, 58
Assumptions. *See* Family cultural lens; Professional cultural lens

Attunement. *See* Learning the family
Aubin, T., 95

Bagnato, S., 17
Bagnaton, S., 5
Bailey, D., 56, 57
Bainter, S., 71, 72, 73
Baker, C., 1, 38, 39
Balance of power. *See* Power: balance
Barrera, I., 4, 13, 15, 41, 59, 61, 85, 96
Bartlett, D. J., 100, 102
Barton, E., 1, 17, 38, 39
Beegle, G., 88
Beneke, M., 41, 59, 83, 85, 95
Benner, L., 1, 38, 39
Bernardo, Kat (contr.), 10, 47–51
Bernheimer, L. P., 4, 22, 27, 28
Bethune, L., 19
Birth to Three System, 10
Block, S. R., 72
Blue-Banning, M., 28, 88
Bornstein, M., 28
Boyce, G., 1, 41, 56
Boyce, L., 3, 39
Boyd, B., 17
Bronfenbrenner, U., 28, 54, 56
Bronson, K., 3, 5
Brooks-Gunn, J., 56
Brotherson, M. J., 22, 41, 43, 44, 60
Brown, J., 16, 38
Bruder, M., 84, 85, 86
Bruton, A. K., 69–70, 71, 72, 73, 82, 83
Bryan, M., 57, 61
Building engagement, 13–15
Busch-Rossnagel, N., 17

Campbell, Erin (contr.), 11, 99, 104–105, 107–113

Campbell, P. H., 3, 38
Campbell, R., 116
Caring attitude, 41–43, 48, 51, 70
Carlson, V., 14
Carroll, D. W., 69–70, 71, 72, 73, 84, 85
Carta, J., 1, 2, 56, 105
Casey, A., 5, 6, 96
Center-based programs, 39
Chang, H.-J., 100
Chard, G., 3, 5, 39, 41, 42, 46
Chazan-Cohen, R., 56
Cheatham, G., 41, 44, 59, 83, 85, 95, 96
Chiarello, L. A., 100, 102
Child development, 1, 13–15, 14, 27, 55, 67
Child learning characteristics, 2, 102
Child learning strategies, 1, 101–105, 102–103, 107, 108
Childress, D. C., 69–70, 71–72, 83, 86
Child's communication needs, 56, 108
Child's perspective, 106–107
Chironis, M., 1, 38, 39
Choice, 46
Cholewa, B., 3
Christensen, L. M., 69, 71, 82, 83
Clarà, M., 8
Coaching models of intervention, 2–4, 18, 30–34, 35, 59
Cohn, E., 2, 5, 28, 56, 100, 105
Collaboration, 5, 74–76, 79–82, 106–107, 117
Commonalities, 14–15
Communication, 29–31, 36, 46, 48, 50, 63, 70–71, 79–82, 122
Community, 2, 24
Compatibility of strategies with family culture, 45
Competence in parenting. *See* Parenting competence
Complexity of early intervention, 1, 3–4
Compromise, 70, 71
Confidence in parenting skills, 1–2, 3, 5, 32, 33–34, 71–72, 99
Conflict resolution plan, 70, 71
Connection, 54, 67
Conroy, M., 18

Consensus building, 87
Constructive feedback, 73
Context of intervention, 16
Contingent responsiveness, 102
Contributions to the field, 86
Contributors to the current work, 9–11. *See also by name*
Coogle, C. G., 69–70, 72, 88
Cook, B. G., 15, 17, 18, 19, 56
Cook, G. A., 1, 2, 3, 39, 56, 105
Cook, S. C., 17, 19
Copeland, C., 3
Cornelius, K., 8
Cornwell, J., 59
Coster, W., 2, 5, 28, 100, 105
Council for Exceptional Children, 2, 16
Cox, J., 18
Creativity, 33, 34
Criticality of partnership, 7
Csikszentmihalyi, M., 60
Cultural context, 4–5, 28, 116
Cultural lens. *See* Family cultural lens; Professional cultural lens
Cultural practices, 4–5, 12, 14–15, 17, 29
Curran, C., 8

DaSilva Iddings, A., 100, 113
Davis, M., 59
Deci, E., 60
Deepening understanding, 6, 19–21, 99, 107–113
Deficit language, 54–55
DeJong, K., 5, 6, 96
DeLap, Cara (contr.), 10, 61, 64–67
Delgado, Benny (contr.), 11, 69, 73–75, 79–82
Denmark, N., 3
Designing interventions, 104–105, 111–112
Developing competencies, 86, 106–107, 108–109
Developmental promotion, 55
Diamond, K., 28
Diegelmann, K., 19
Dinnebeil, L., 5, 53, 59, 60–61
Direct teaching, 14
Disabilities, 57, 71

Index

Di Santo, A., 100, 103, 110
Disciplinary expertise. *See* Professional expertise
Division for Early Childhood (DEC), 2, 3, 15, 27, 29, 83
Dodici, B., 56
Dokecki, P., 61
Doran, P., 88
Draper, D., 56
Dunst, C. J., 1, 2, 3, 6, 8, 16, 17, 18, 28, 39, 42, 45, 46, 54, 56, 57, 59, 60–61, 94, 99, 100, 105, 119
Dworkin, P., 112
Dynamic partnerships, 116

Early Head Start, 56
Early Intervention Guidebook for Families and Professionals (Keilty), 1, 2, 119
Early intervention professionals. *See* Professionals
Early Intervention Program, 119
EBP (evidence-based practice). *See* Evidence-based practice (EBP)
Edelen-Smith, P. J., 18
Educational rights, 2
Edwards, P. A., 95
Effectiveness, 1–2, 15–19, 57
Efficacy. *See* Effectiveness
EI (early intervention) professionals. *See* Professionals
Emotions, 21–22, 41–42, 110
Empathy, 42
Empowerment, 49, 51, 59, 63, 67, 70
Engagement, 2–3, 5, 29, 38–39, 40. *See also* Levels of participation
Engster, D., 60
Enrollment in early intervention, 39
Ephphatha Consulting Services, 11
Epley, P., 22, 41, 43, 44, 57, 60
Equal partners. *See* Power: balance
Erwin, E., 5, 53, 57, 59, 60–61, 66, 83, 84, 85, 88, 102
Eshbaugh, E., 38, 44, 45
Espe-Sherwindt, M., 3, 18, 45, 46, 54, 94
Espinosa, L., 13, 27, 28, 29, 30, 41, 58, 95

Ethical caring, 42
Ethnic practices. *See* Cultural practices
Etschiedt, S., 8
Evaluation. *See* Assessment
Evans, D. L., 70, 72
Evidence-based practice (EBP), 12, 15–19, 25–26
Expectations, 14, 44, 45. *See also* Family cultural lens; Professional cultural lens
Expert power, 58, 66

Family competencies. *See* Family strengths
Family cultural lens, 13–15, 19–21
Family identity. *See* Family cultural lens
Family interactions, 15, 25, 30, 67, 80, 81
Family knowledge base. *See* Funds of knowledge
Family–professional partnership (FPP)
 and culture, 29–30
 essential concepts, 4–7
 importance in early intervention, 3–4, 7, 116–117
Family quality of life, 57
Family strengths, 102–105, 109–110. *See also* Parenting competence
Family Strengths in Child Learning (FamSCL) (Keilty & Galvin), 102, 104
Family-systems intervention, 2–4
Family values
 and engagement, 43–45, 48
 parenting, 12–15, 24–25, 27–29
 and partnering, 4–5, 6, 29–30, 30–37, 86, 116, 117
Federal policy, 119–120
Feedback, 29, 36, 73, 81, 116, 119
Feit, M. D., 70, 72
Feller, N., 100, 113
Fewell, R., 56
Fialka, J., 41, 42, 95, 96, 97, 117
Fidelity to evidence, 16, 17–18
Fielder, J., 5, 6, 96
Fiese, B., 104
Fingerhut, P. E., 116
Fiss, A., 100

Fit
  and cultural context, 13, 56
  family/child to intervention, 6, 23–26, 36, 37, 108, 112–113, 115, 117–118
  therapist to family, 81–82, 108–110
Fleming, J., 3
Flexibility, 16, 18, 55, 119
Flores, M. M., 69–70
Flow with the family, 20–21, 22
Foley, G., 43
Follow-up discussions, 32
Formality, 30
Fowler, R., 60
Fox, L., 56, 57
FPP (family–professional partnership). *See* Family–professional partnership (FPP)
Fraiberg, L., 42–43
Framing, 55
Frankland, H. C., 88
Freund, M., 56
Friend, A., 22, 41, 43, 44, 60
Friesen, A., 13, 14
Funding, 119–120
Funds of knowledge, 99–101, 103, 110

Gallagher, P., 57, 59, 96, 97
Gallimore, R., 4, 27, 28
Galvin, K., 3, 5–6, 28, 56, 100, 102, 103, 104, 112
Gauvain, M., 27
Gauvreau, A., 17
Geller, E., 43
Gender biases, 71
Generalization, 40
Gerlach-Downie, S., 3, 39, 40
Gestural communication, 14, 29
Gewell, R., 1
Ghaly, Marian (contr.), 10, 30–36
Gilkerson, L., 42–43
Goal setting. *See* Agreeing on strategies/goals
Godfrey, E., 13, 22
González, N., 99, 100, 111
Goodness of fit. *See* Fit
Griffith, E., 57
Grolnick, W., 60

Guerette, A. R., 69–70, 72, 88
Guralnick, M. J., 17, 28, 57
Guthrie, D., 28

Hadidi, M. S., 29
Halle, T., 119
Hamby, D., 1, 2, 3, 6, 8, 39, 42, 56, 57, 99, 100, 105
Hanline, M. F., 69–70, 72, 88
Hanson, M., 13, 14, 15, 27, 28, 29, 30, 41, 58, 95
Hansuvadha, N., 69–70, 96, 97
Harbin, G. L., 59
Harn, B., 16, 18
Harper, Rashonda (contr.), 10, 47–49, 51
Harry, B., 15, 35, 41, 44, 58, 61, 66
Hart, H., 1
Harwood, R., 14
Hauser-Cram, P., 1
Hebbeler, C., 3
Heffron, M., 41, 43, 45
Help My Baby Learn (Mitchell), 11
Hepburn, S., 57
Herlders, P., 1
Hernandez, F., 39, 40
Hinton, V., 69–70
Historical biases, 71
Hitt, S., 19
Honesty. *See* Openness
Hulleman, C., 16, 17
Hunter, C., 13, 22
Hurwitz, S., 1, 38, 39
Hypothesizing. *See* Trying things out

Implementing evidence-based practice, 16–17
Inclusion of family members, 25
Individualization, 7–8, 17, 58, 103, 105, 112, 117–118
Individualized Family Service Plan (IFSP), 53
Individuals with Disabilities Education Act (IDEA), 119
Informed decision making, 2, 59
Innocenti, M. S., 1, 2, 56, 105
Institute of Medicine, 28, 56
Institutional power, 58, 66, 67

Integration of information and strategies, 40
Interpretation of the evidence base, 12–13
Interpreter services, 70
Interventionist-directed practices, 3
Intervention time with family, 25, 80, 81
Involved level of engagement, 39
Ivins, B., 41, 43, 45

James, C., 3, 5, 39, 41, 42, 46
Jayaraman, G., 71, 72, 73
Jeffries, L., 100
Jeon, H., 38, 44, 45
Jimenez, T. R., 69, 70, 71, 82
Johnson, M., 2, 56, 105
Johnson II, Benton (contr.), 10, 19, 21–25
Jones-Harden, B., 3
Jump, V., 3, 39
Jung, L. A., 54, 94

Kahanna-Kalman, R., 14, 15
Kalyanpur, M., 15, 35, 41, 44, 58, 61, 66
Karst, J., 57
Kärtner, J., 4, 14, 27
Kaufman, S., 4, 27, 28
Keilty, B., 1, 3, 5–6, 28, 41, 43, 56, 57, 71, 86, 94, 100, 102, 103, 104, 112, 119
Kellar-Guenther, Y., 72, 73
Kellegrew, D., 28
Keller, H., 4, 14, 27
Kelley, S., 57
Kemp, P., 3
Kemp-Inman, A., 19
Kennedy, J., 39
Keogh, B. K., 4, 22, 28
Ketelaar, M., 1
Khetani, M., 2, 5, 28, 56, 100, 105
Kilgo, J. L., 69–70, 71, 72, 73, 82, 83
Kim, J. M., 56
King, G. A., 100
Kingsley, K., 38, 39
Knoche, L., 71, 72, 73
Kondrich, Kurt (contr.), 10, 21–25

Kong, N., 1, 2, 56, 105
Kontos, S., 28
Kramer, L., 4, 13, 15, 41, 59, 61, 85, 96
Krauss, M. W., 59, 60
Kresak, K., 57
Kyzar, K., 22, 41, 43, 44, 60

LaForme Fiss, A., 100
Lalvani, P., 85, 96, 97
Language, 54–55
Language learning, 2
Law, M., 2, 5, 28, 100, 105
Lawji, D., 116
Leadership skills, 2
Leaps and Bounds Family Services, 11
Learning the family, 23, 25, 31–32, 76–77, 79
Leavell, A., 14, 15
Ledford, J., 16, 18
Lee, Y. H., 41, 57, 69, 70, 71, 72, 83, 88
Lessons learned
  collaboration/communication, 79–82
  deepening understanding, 108–113
  parenting and partnership, 34–37, 47–51
  power, 66–67
  teaming test, 93–97
  ways of knowing and making decisions, 21–26
Levels of participation, 39–40
Lewis, C., 116
Lieberman-Betz, R., 16
Linn, M. I., 39, 40
Listening, 47–48, 63
Llagas, C., 88
Long-term focus, 73
Luo, R., 14, 15
Luze, G., 38, 44, 45
Lynch, E., 13, 15, 29, 41

Macpherson, T. D., 4, 13, 15, 41, 59, 61, 85, 96
Macy, M., 17
Mahoney, G., 1, 6, 41, 56
Mailloux, Z., 38, 39
Martin, K., 13, 14

Martinez, N., 116
Martinez-Beck, I., 119
Marvin, C., 71, 72, 73
Maul, C., 4, 27, 28
Mazur, A., 88
McCollum, J., 38
McConnell, S., 17
McInerney, W., 5, 53, 59, 60–61
McLeod, B., 18
McWayne, C., 39
McWilliam, P. J., 35, 36, 41, 54, 59, 60–61, 83, 85, 86, 88, 93, 94
McWilliam, R. A., 4, 5, 6, 14–15, 17, 39, 41, 43, 54, 59, 72, 73, 84, 96, 111, 118
Mechanisms for acquiring knowledge, 22–23
Melzi, G., 39
Metz, A., 119
Minke, K., 41
Misunderstandings, 71
Mitchell, Jamie (contr.), 11, 90, 93–97
Mixon, K., 3
Modifications, 112–113
Moll, L., 99, 100, 110
Moore, H., 1, 38, 39
Morgese, Z., 2, 14, 56, 105
Mortenson, P., 95
Multiple relationships, 80–81
Multiple strategies, 25–26
Mundt, K., 39
Mutual respect, 117
Mutual support, 86

Nagro, S., 8
Naig, L., 22, 41, 43, 44, 60
Najar, Judith (contr.), 10, 61–64, 66–67
National Academies of Sciences, Engineering, and Medicine, 13, 14, 17, 22, 41, 56, 57
Navigating the intervention system, 59
"Needs" versus "weaknesses," 54–55
Neisworth, J., 5
Nelson, L. L., 88
Ng, F., 13, 22
Nieves, Barbara (contr.), 10, 30–36
Nihira, K., 28
Noddings, N., 42

Nonchronological engagement path, 40
Nonjudgmental attitude, 70
Nonlinear engagement path, 40
Nonverbal communication, 14, 29
Novak, I., 100

Objectivity, 78, 80, 81
Object play, 14–15
Observation, 25, 103–104
Odom, S. L., 15, 17, 18
Olson, B. D., 69, 70, 71, 82
One-up perspective, 19–20
Open-ended assessment, 55
Openness, 7, 29, 70, 81–82
Optimism, 72, 73
Organization of book, 9
Orsmond, G., 2, 5, 28, 100, 105
Outcomes, 13, 14

Palisano, R. J., 100, 102
Parental well-being, 2
Parenting capacities. See Family strengths; Parenting competence
Parenting competence, 1, 2, 3, 71–72, 76, 85, 99. See also Family strengths
Parenting practices research, 14–15
Parenting skills. See Parenting competence
Parenting strategies, 13, 26–27
Parenting style, 35, 104
Parents as Teachers home-visiting program, 39
Parisi, D., 16, 18
Park, J., 28
Participation. See Engagement
Partner interactions, 29–30
Partnership concepts, 4–6
Partnership design, 3–4
Partnership themes, 116–117
Passive participation, 39
Pelletier, J., 100, 103, 110
Perales, F., 6
Perspective, 19–20, 46, 102
Pestel, Michèle (contr.), 11, 89–91, 93–95
Peterson, C., 38, 44, 45, 56
Pierce, D., 28

Index

Piro, J., 116
Planning an intervention strategy, 73, 104, 109–110
Play, 14–15, 31
Policy, 119–120
Porter, A., 59, 60–61, 70, 72, 73
Positive encouragement to child, 76, 81
Positive perception, 54–55, 66, 70
Power. *See also* Empowerment
　about, 53
　balance of, 5, 6, 20–21, 60–62, 66–67, 70, 85, 117
　of child, 56–57
　family, 5, 54–57, 64, 66, 76, 77, 88
　institutional, 58, 66, 67
　lessons, 66–67
　professional, 6, 58–60, 64
　reflections on, 63–65
　and role, 60
Practice toolbox, 19
Present-and-available level of engagement, 39
Pretti-Frontczak, K., 17
Primacy of family, 88–89
Prioritizing family concerns, 48–49
Privacy, 50
Privileged position, 50, 66, 120
Process nature of early intervention, 106, 118
Professional cultural lens, 4, 13, 15
Professional development, 15, 19
Professional expertise, 12, 67, 84–85, 119
Professionals
　attitudes/beliefs, 4, 13, 69, 116
　as family, 117
　and flexibility, 46
　perspective of, 35–36, 117
　and power, 6, 58–60, 64
　and practice, 1–2
　strengths and needs of, 66–67
Promoting engagement, 40–46

Quality of interactions, 54, 56
Quality of life, 66
Questions for reflection, 26, 37, 52, 68, 82, 98, 114

Raab, M., 1, 2, 16, 18, 28, 56, 99, 105
Rahn, N., 17
Raikes, H., 56
Raspa, M., 56, 57
Rationale, 95–96
Raver, S. A., 69–70, 71–72, 83, 86
Readiness to engage, 40–41, 51
Reciprocity, 85, 112
Recommended practices, 2, 3–4, 119–120
Reed, S. F., 69, 70, 71, 82
Reflections
　collaboration, 74–79
　communication, 76–79
　deepening understanding, 19–21, 106–109
　engagement, 47–51
　power, 61–65
　teaming, 89–93
Reflective practice, 6, 8–9, 19–21, 118–119
Regulations, 119–120
Reichow, B., 16, 17
Relational practices, 2–3, 48
Relevance, 44
Research in early intervention, 1–2
Research on parenting practices, 14–15
Resistance to change, 21
Resources, 2, 15, 19
Respect, 3, 29, 70, 71
Responsive caregiving, 56
Responsive partnering, 3, 29, 30–34, 35, 36–37, 118
Responsive practice, 15
Revision, 22–23, 25, 36
Reyes, I., 100, 113
Rhodes, C., 96, 97
Ridgely, R., 73
Rimm-Kaufman, S., 16, 17
Robinson, C. C., 6, 72
Rodin, G., 60
Roggman, L. S., 1, 2, 3, 39, 56, 105
Role in partnership, 36–37, 63, 66, 67
Role-power conflicts, 60
Rosenberg, S. A., 72
Ross Kantz, K., 38, 44, 45
Routine activities, 4–5, 27–28, 31–32, 34, 72, 101–107, 109–110

Rowley, P., 5, 6, 96
Rush, D., 8, 18, 36, 84, 86, 88, 100
Ryan, R., 60

Safe atmosphere, 43
Salisbury, C., 3
Sameroff, A., 104
Sandall, S., 17
Santagata, R., 8, 118
Santos, R., 44, 83, 96
Sass-Lehrer, M., 59, 60–61, 70, 72, 73
Saul, D., 3
Sawyer, B., 3
Sawyer, C., 8
Sawyer, L. B., 38
SBIs (strengths-based interventions). *See* Strengths-based interventions (SBIs)
Scaffolding, 14–15
Schertz, H., 1, 38, 39
Schick, A., 39
Schiffman, R., 56
Schmidt, M. M., 18
Schwartz, I., 17
Scott, M., 41
Self-efficacy, 57
Self-reflection, 22
Seligman, M., 60
Sensitive practices, 51
Sensitivity, 61, 70, 75, 102
Seven essential partnership concepts, 4–6
Sewell, T., 3
Sexton, D., 17
Shamoon-Shanok, R., 42–43
Shared expectations, 43–44
Sharing the evidence base, 22–23
Shelden, M., 8, 18, 36, 84, 86, 88, 100
Shifts and modifications, 118
Shippen, M., 69–70
Shogren, K., 5, 53, 57, 59, 60–61, 66, 83, 84, 85, 88, 102
Shonkoff, J. P., 1
Simkus, A., 1, 2, 56, 105
Singer, G., 4, 27, 28
Smaller, B., 12
Smith, C. M., 69, 70, 71, 82
Smith, G. J., 18

Smyth, C., 2, 14, 56, 105
Snyder, P., 73
Sokoly, M., 61
Song, L., 14, 15
Soodak, L., 5, 53, 57, 59, 60–61, 66, 83, 84, 85, 88, 102
Specialized education and training, 58
Spicer, C., 2, 14, 56, 105
Spicer, P., 14
Spiker, D., 1, 39, 40, 41, 56
Spino, M., 5, 53, 59, 60–61
Stoner, T., 100
Stoolmiller, M., 16, 18
Strengths-based interventions (SBIs), 54–55, 96, 99–100
Stress/anxiety, 78
Strozier, S. D., 69–70
Summers, J. A., 22, 41, 43, 44, 57, 60, 88
Sutherland, K., 18
Sutton, A., 116
Swanson, J., 28, 99
Systems influencers, 119–120

Taggart, G., 8
Tamis-LeMonda, C., 13, 14, 15, 22
Taylor, S., 69–70
Teaming. *See also* Partnership
 equality of members, 84–87, 88
 and inclusivity, 87–88
 and leadership, 86
 lessons learned, 93–97
 primacy of family, 88–89
 recommendations, 83
 reflections on, 32–33, 89–93
 research findings, 83–84
 spirit of, 6
Technology use, 46
Test, D., 19
Testing. *See* Trying things out
Themes for successful intervention, 6
Therapist/therapy, 74
Thinking outside the box, 33, 34
Timmons, K., 100, 103, 110
Traditional practice, 3
Transactional nature, 117
Transitions, 113

Trent, T., 70, 72
Trivette, C. M., 1, 2, 3, 6, 8, 16, 17, 18, 28, 39, 42, 45, 54, 56, 57, 59, 60–61, 99, 100, 105
Trust, 3, 7, 19, 29, 50–51, 69, 79, 110–111, 117
Trying things out, 39, 73, 78–79, 117
Turbiville, V., 28
Turnbull, A., 3, 5, 22, 28, 41, 43, 44, 53, 57, 59, 60–61, 66, 83, 84, 85, 88, 102
Turnbull, R., 5, 53, 57, 59, 60–61, 66, 83, 84, 85, 88, 102

Understanding. *See* Deepening understanding
Understanding the intervention, 43–44
Unequal power, 60–61
Universals, 14–15
Unproven practice, 17

Van Hecke, A., 57
Verbal communication, 14
Vermeer, A., 1
Viola, J. J., 69, 70, 71, 82
Vision, 13

Votava, K., 5, 6, 96

Wagner, M., 39, 40
Wainer, A., 57
Ways of being. *See* Family cultural lens; Professional cultural lens
Ways of knowing, 4, 19–21
Ways of parenting, 13, 26–27
Weisner, T. S., 4, 22, 28
Westcott, S., 102
Weston, D., 41, 43, 45
Wheeden, C., 1, 56
Whole-family engagement, 50–51, 107
Williams, G., 60
Wilson, A., 8
Wolery, M., 16, 18, 73, 79
Wolsfeld, Jen (contr.), 10–11, 80–82
Woods, J., 3, 16, 38
Wu, C. L., 59, 60–61, 70, 72, 73

Yahya, R., 73
Yates, T., 38
Ylitapio-Mäntylä, O., 60
Yoshikawa, H., 13, 14, 15, 22

Zhang, X., 56

About the Authors

Bonnie Keilty, EdD, has worked in early intervention for over 20 years as a practitioner, university instructor, professional development provider, and researcher. She is an associate professor in the Special Education Department at Hunter College in New York City. She coordinates Hunter's Early Childhood Special Education program. Bonnie's work focuses on early intervention practices that support the family in their parenting role and promote infant–toddler development, and prepare professionals to provide that support. Her first book, *The Early Intervention Guidebook for Families and Professionals,* has been used across the country to support families and emerging and current professionals in understanding the vision for early intervention. Bonnie is a former president of the Division for Early Childhood of the Council for Exceptional Children.

Hedi Levine, MSEd, began her work in early intervention in 1992 after the birth of her daughter. The partnerships she forged propelled her into the professional world of infant and parent development, which she studied at Bank Street College of Education in New York City. She has worked as an early interventionist, a supervisor of early childhood teachers in home- and community-based programs, and as a group and workshop leader for families and educators. Hedi's own experiences and those of parents and professionals she encounters continue to guide her. She is currently completing her doctorate in social welfare at the Silberman School of Social Work through the Graduate Center at the City University of New York.

Sagarika Kosaraju, EdD, served as visiting assistant professor at Hunter College, City University of New York (CUNY), teaching courses on authentic assessment, literacy, and student teaching. Sagarika has a doctorate from The George Washington University in special education, where she also served as a graduate research assistant for the Department of Special Education and Disability Studies. Her dissertation was in partnership with Early Stages, a division of the District of Columbia Public Schools, to analyze timeframes and family factors related to parent participation in the eligibility determination process for preschool children. Sagarika was a special educator for 6 years in early childhood special education and taught in a variety of environments, including homes, classrooms, and community inclusion settings.